# MAYDAY!

## YACHTS IN DISTRESS

# MAYDAY!

## YACHTS IN DISTRESS

Joachim Schult

Translated by Detlef Jens

ADLARD COLES NAUTICAL
London

# CONTENTS

Published by Adlard Coles Nautical 1997
an imprint of A&C Black (Publishers) Ltd
35 Bedford Row, London WC1R 4JH

First published 1993 in Germany by Delius Klasing Verlag,
Siekerwall 21, D-33602 Bielefeld, Germany
with the title *Mayday: Yachten in Seenot*

ISBN 0-7136-4642-X

A CIP catalogue record for this book is available from the British
Library.

Typeset in 10½/12½pt Sabon by SPAN Graphics Limited
Printed and bound in Great Britain by
Bell & Bain Limited, Glasgow

**Photocredits**
The following is a list of photographers whose work is featured in
the colour sections of this book. Figures in brackets indicate the number
of photos supplied:
Bartels (3), Behn (2), Hörmann (3), Koppelmann (3), Mastmeier (2),
Mepmer (1), Mendlowitz/Callahan (2), Mertes (2), Niemann (2),
Norddeutsche Versicherungs-Gesellschaft (12), Pantaenius (3),
Pardy (6), Photographic Department (1), Pickthall (1), Dr Pohlan (2),
Stendel/Kalipke (2), Suhr (3), Thompson Newspaper (2),
Joachim Schult (1), *Yacht* magazine (3).

All the black and white photographs are from the
author's collection (17).

The line drawings are by van Straaten.

# INTRODUCTION

*The sea is merciless. It never shows sympathy for human feelings. Anyone with hopeful romantic notions of trusting in the mercy of Poseidon will soon get a bitter reminder of the complete and uncompromising indifference with which the winds and the sea hand out favours and misfortunes.*

*Hans Domizlaff*

The accidents described in this book reflect the realities of contemporary yachting, especially cruising, in coastal and off-shore waters. Most of the incidents speak for themselves.

But I do not want to talk about sailing accidents in a general or sentimental way. Nor do I want to sound patronizing or accusing. What I want to do, though, is to deal with authentic accounts of accidents. The descriptions of incidents on the following pages are edited versions of documentary reports, sometimes supplemented by information on meteorology, maritime law, pilotage (taken from the relevant publications), yacht construction and other nautical topics.

The reader can verify facts and statements and draw his own conclusions from personal experience of, say, a particular area or type of boat.

The stories are based on the first-hand reports of those concerned, on statements made in court, on written accounts or other documents. Sometimes they had to be edited, shortened or added to.

It is not the objective of the book to apportion blame for the accidents described. But the summary and assessment of several incidents together serve to point to the causes of accidents.

The real names of people and their boats involved are used if they have agreed to publication, if they have already been published elsewhere, or if police, coastguard or other organizations have passed the names on. In other cases the names of people and boats have been changed.

However, the details of accidents and their locations are never changed as the circumstances of a distress situation are vital for understanding what actually happened. This is particularly true of meteorological and navigational data.

Also unchanged are the names of vessels and persons who rendered assistance, as these are a matter of record and, besides, they deserve recognition for their actions.

In the ordering of the material I have tried not only to group the incidents by type (eg man overboard, sinking), but also to emphasize links in terms of date or geographical area. This could be the basis of a more systematic study of yachting accidents than is currently available, although for that a much more comprehensive survey would be needed.

Any research of this nature should not stop at collecting raw facts, but should also take into account contributory factors. I believe that the reader of this book will arrive at the same conclusion as myself: that nearly all incidents described here are, in the final analysis, the result of human error. I believe that it is wrong to blame sailing accidents solely on circumstances such as weather. Most of the accidents in this book could have been avoided, had not someone somewhere along the line taken the wrong decision. Some of the errors could have been spotted not only after the accident but also before the event if the crews had shown a little bit more nautical common sense.

I quote from a guide for the training of young sailors concerning the 'prudence of a good skipper': 'The personality of a good and prudent skipper combines 10 per cent knowledge, 40 per cent experience, 49 per cent caution and 1 per cent daring.' This book does not aim to be a textbook, but nevertheless it should illustrate the realities of cruising offshore, spread knowledge and pass on experience. And it should serve as a reminder to be cautious. In short, it should help prevent accidents at sea.

Not all skippers and crews are quick to recognize dangers and potential problems at sea. Recognition comes through knowledge of past accidents and is enhanced by relating them to particular circumstances such as time, place and weather. In this book I aim to show these interrelationships, because nearly every accident has not one cause, but several.

Good seamanship means always being prudent; one can never rely on being rescued!

On board *Cormoran*
JOACHIM SCHULT

# 1
# MAN OVERBOARD

---

## *Family tragedies*

*Every year quite a few yachtsmen lose their lives
as a result of falling overboard. Nevertheless
very few sailors take the obvious precaution of
wearing a harness. The following two cases
made a deep impression on the author and have
had a lasting influence on his attitude to safety.*

For most yachtsmen the cry 'Man overboard' does not mean
that a potentially fatal accident has occurred but is just the
signal for a bit of fun with a fender on a Sunday afternoon, or
even just a heading in a sailing manual.

Sadly, most people will only really start to take proper care
on a boat and appreciate the real risks of falling overboard
after they have actually had it happen to themselves and been
lucky enough to be rescued, or have seen it happen to someone
else, or know the fatal consequences of it happening to someone they knew. Most others will probably continue in their
carefree ways, with more or less disregard for danger, until it is
their turn to experience the real thing.

I read about the first tragic case early in my sailing career
and it made such a deep impression on me that I have been
extremely careful ever since when afloat, passing on the same,

some might say pedantic, attitude towards safety years later when first my wife and then my children joined me on the water. The other story is even more sad and made no less an impression, even though it happened many decades later. It is clear that, despite the fact that the two incidents are separated by all those years during which boats have become safer and safety equipment has improved, nothing much has really changed. Yachtsmen have learnt little, if anything, about this aspect of safety.

Only if we accept that falling overboard is very often the result of mere carelessness and that it will very likely mean the death of the person concerned, will we take enough care when moving about on deck and take all the necessary measures to prevent ourselves falling in. But now on to the two cases which shaped my attitude.

The first occurred during a transatlantic race from Newport, Rhode Island, to Bergen in Norway in the year 1935. Five American and one German yacht started on this 3,500 mile race, all of them of course well manned.

The *Hamrah* was a heavy gaff ketch with a length of 54 ft (16.5 m), a beam of 12 ft 2 in (3.7 m) and a draft of 6 ft 6 in (2 m), belonging to the yachtsman Robert R Ames and sailed by him, his two sons, Richard (23) and Henry (20), as well as three other young men. This was the normal size of crew for this yacht where the deck gear was so heavy that each watch had three men and all three were needed for sail changes and other manoeuvres.

On the morning of 19 June when *Hamrah* was in mid-ocean in position roughly 46° N, 40° W, almost exactly midway between the two continents, the disaster occurred. The boat was in heavy seas and taking large quantities of water on her decks. Robert Ames was sitting in the dinghy lashed on deck just abaft the mainmast where he probably felt quite safe from the seas sweeping the decks. Suddenly *Hamrah* was struck by a gust which heeled her far over while at the same time a particularly large sea washed him overboard. The crew had previously rigged lifelines across the deck to hold on to, but Ames was unable to grab one.

The helmsman's urgent cry of 'Man overboard!' brought

the rest of the crew scrambling on deck, headed by the eldest son, Richard. When he saw his father in the water he quickly tied a line around himself and jumped in after him. But the line which would have attached him to the yacht was too short, so without hesitation he untied himself and swam towards his father.

In the meantime the rest of the crew had managed to gybe the heavy ketch and sail her back to the two men in the water. However, the yacht was stopped by heavy seas about a boat's length away and as she began drifting further away all the crew could do was to throw the two men a lifering and bear away for a new attempt to sail up to them. In the gybe that followed, the massive boom broke and *Hamrah* ended up even further away from where father and son had by now been swimming for quite a long time.

In this desperate situation the younger son, Henry, launched the dinghy and rowed across to his father and brother, but when he reached them only his brother was still alive. Their father, who had been wearing oilskins and sea boots when he went over, had already drowned.

As Henry pulled his brother into the dinghy it capsized. Both brothers were now clinging to the dinghy and this was the last that the remaining three men on *Hamrah* ever saw of them.

On board the ketch the young sailor Charles F Tillinghurst had now taken command. The disabled boat with her broken boom had drifted far to leeward and it was only after two hours of hard work that they were able to beat back to the scene of the disaster. But they never sighted either the dinghy or the brothers again, even though they searched the area for many hours. For the next two days they had to lie hove-to and wait for the storm to blow itself out before they could sail the yacht back to the harbour at Sydney on the coast of Newfoundland. For this remarkable feat of seamanship, Tillinghurst was awarded the coveted Blue Water Medal of the Cruising Club of America.

On this sad occasion the Atlantic claimed all three male members of one family. We will not dwell on possible human errors that contributed to this tragedy, but we can ask ourselves whether we would have acted as courageously as the two sons under the same circumstances.

Moreover, we can do everything possible to prevent people falling overboard from our own boats, because then we can forestall the tragic chain of events that befell the crew of the *Hamrah*.

The next story is for all those who think, 'I am an experienced sailor; it could not happen to me.' It too culminates in the North Atlantic, this time in 1985.

Peter Tangvald was one of those enviable people who, while not a rich man, was able to sail the oceans at will, without the need to stop and make money ashore. An American of Norwegian descent, he was only happy when he was sailing. However, a series of misfortunes marred what otherwise would have been an idyllic lifestyle.

Towards the end of a five year circumnavigation he lost his 32 ft (9.8 m) cruiser *Dorothea* after colliding with an unidentified floating object off Barbados in 1967. He had to abandon his sinking yacht and covered 50 miles in his tiny dinghy to reach the small Caribbean island of Cannouan.

Several years later, he purchased the 49 ft (15 m) centreboard gaff cutter *L'Artemis de Pytheas*, married a young French girl, Lydia, and set off on a new world cruise, this time from Europe through the Red Sea and the Indian Ocean to the China Sea. On the voyage their son, Thomas, was born on board in the middle of the Indian Ocean and miles from any coast. This caused great bureaucratic trouble later as the child had no official birth certificate because he was born at sea with only his parents present and neither a doctor nor a midwife to witness the birth. Matters went so far that the little boy was nearly taken away from his father.

Tragically, Thomas' mother, Lydia, was killed during an attack by pirates in the Sea of Sulu on 10 February 1979. The fact that he was holding his son at the time was apparently the only reason that Tangvald himself was not murdered by the pirates. So Tangvald experienced the joy of becoming a father at sea only to become a widower just a few months later.

So he was alone with his son and his boat. Not long afterwards he met Ann, a young Malaysian woman, who joined them in their seafaring life and came to assume the role of mother to Thomas and wife to Tangvald. It proved to be a very remarkable and romantic relationship.

On her return to western waters the yacht was again attacked by pirates, this time at Gabes on the Tunisian coast. By threatening to rape Ann, the pirates got away with every last penny on the boat.

The following morning the couple had a conversation that Tangvald may have had occasion to ponder later.

'Suppose the pirates had killed me,' Ann mused, 'you could have had a serious problem, Peter. Can you be sure that the police would have accepted your story? I would have been the second woman to have died mysteriously on your boat within just two years. You would probably have been suspected of murder, maybe of being a mental case who kills his partners and invents stories about pirates as a cover.'

'Yes, it could have been a problem,' Peter admitted.

In fact it is a horrific scenario which might in theory befall any blue water cruising yacht with a crew of two. If one of the two dies at sea, burial at sea becomes imperative after a few days. Then people could start wondering about murder. A loud argument, perhaps, in the last port of call overheard by others, might arouse nasty suspicions.

But on board *L'Artemis de Pytheas* happiness reigned once more after this traumatic incident. They sail to the Caribbean where Ann and Peter marry on Martinique in 1982. A halcyon time follows and a year later they have a baby, about which Tangvald tells friends in a letter written as if by the child:

My name is Carmen Tangvald. I was born seven weeks ago here in Portugal, but my life really had its beginning nine months earlier on Martinique. Since then we have cruised the Caribbean and sailed across the Atlantic to Europe. We, that is my father Peter, my mother Ann and my half-brother Thomas, anchored in the lagoon of Faro in southern Portugal which we reached in our boat just prior to my birth, as I had heard that Faro is a very good place for little girls to be born.

13

Before my birth the labour pains set in very late and I think my father established a new world record for rowing a ten-foot dinghy as he had to take my mother ashore and to hospital as quickly as possible. If I have understood the sometimes confusing conversations of my parents correctly, I believe that they did not want a repetition of the problem of my brother Thomas who was born at sea without an official birth certificate. Such pieces of paper seem to mean so much in this world, even though my brother looks just like a miniature version of my father and it should be instantly clear to anyone that these two are father and son.

The Tangvald family, now four strong, stayed in Portugal for the winter and spring. Then, they set sail to the Canary Islands and in early 1985 embarked on yet another Atlantic passage back to the Caribbean. On their way to Martinique, where Peter and Ann had been married, with Carmen on board who was now one and a half years old (exactly the same age as her brother Thomas was when his mother died on the same deck), tragedy occurred.

'It was 26 January 1985 and we were sailing west before a fresh trade wind. After breakfast Ann went on deck to wash the nappies, as she did every day, while I went into the forepeak to play with the children. After a while I followed Ann on deck to help her.

'She had just finished with the washing and had started to hang the nappies up on a line when I noticed that the line was a bit too close to the wind-vane and was interfering with it. The boat had just started to veer away from her correct course. Before I had time to remove the line so that the wind-vane would bring her back on course, the boat bore away further and gybed. I shouted a warning to Ann to duck beneath the boom as it swung across, but too late. Before she could react the heavy boom had hit her and catapulted her right over the side. At the same time the boat heeled alarmingly and headed up into the wind.

'Although it took me only a few seconds to bring the boat right around and stop her I had already lost sight of Ann. My eight-year-old son Thomas had by now come on deck and helped me to sail the boat while we searched for Ann for more than six hours. But we never saw her again. Probably she was knocked unconscious instantly when the boom hit her and drowned.'

Everyone will probably be able to imagine at least some of Tangvald's feelings, having found happiness and lost it again on the deck of his *L'Artemis de Pytheas* twice within a short period of his life. He was suddenly alone again, now with the eight-year-old Thomas and the not quite two-year-old Carmen, a lonely figure who had also lost his love of this boat and even of sailing itself.

• • • • • • •

# Danger on all sides

*Anyone falling overboard from a yacht at sea, or sometimes even one in harbour, is in real danger. If he goes overboard, even the most capable sailor is reduced to passivity, while those left on board can face a daunting task in trying to rescue him.*

Naomi James, the first woman to sail around the world single-handed, once said, 'I have never believed that the sea can be good or bad. The sea is just a vast mass of water without feeling, hate or sympathy.'

But the risk of drowning is ever present when we are on the water, not just out at sea. And it can happen to anyone, even the most experienced of sailors. This awful truth was brought home by the death of one of the most successful offshore skippers of his time, Rob James, Naomi's husband, who had raced more than 100,000 miles across some of the roughest oceans in the world. When lowering the sails on his trimaran just outside Salcombe harbour, he fell into the water and drowned.

Rob James was then 36 years old. After having studied maths and information sciences he worked as a charter skipper in the Canary Islands for Chay Blyth. Later, in 1974, he was skipper of the 72 ft (22 m) ketch *Second Life* in the Whitbread Race. In the next Whitbread he raced again across the Southern Ocean, this time on Blyth's *Great Britain II*. Again with Blyth, he won the Round Britain Race on the trimaran *Great Britain IV*. In 1980 he competed in the singlehanded transatlantic race in a multihull. In 1981 he won, again with Chay Blyth, the Two Star race across the Atlantic. In 1982 he again won the Round Britain.

How could such an experienced sailor drown just outside his home port on the south coast of England? In March 1983 he was sailing the large trimaran *Colt Cars GB* to Salcombe for a thorough refit before the start of that year's racing season. One of the items at the top of the list to be fixed was the netting between the hulls. This was strong and hard-wearing, but the boat had been sailed hard for several months and now signs of wear and tear were noticeable.

As James took down the foresail on the narrow foredeck in the entrance to Salcombe harbour he lost his balance and stepped on to the net, which broke immediately so that he fell between the hulls into the water. His cry of 'Overboard' alerted the crew, Jeffrey Houlgrave, who was asleep in his bunk. He dashed on deck and threw James a horseshoe lifebuoy which fell far short of him. Precious seconds had already been lost and the large trimaran was fast even under the one remaining foresail.

The yacht was a racing machine and did not have an engine. It was difficult for Houlgrave to manoeuvre the big tri back against the tide under the one foresail. Four desperate attempts to get James back on board failed. Sometimes the large yacht stopped only 20 yards away from James; sometimes it stopped much further away. In despair Houlgrave finally jumped overboard himself and swam over to the now seriously cold and nearly unconscious James, but he was unable to get him back on board. It was only with great difficulty that Houlgrave himself managed to climb back on deck, sail the trimaran into the harbour and alert the rescue services.

Forty minutes after he had fallen in, a helicopter found James in the sea, but he was already dead from hypothermia and drowning.

In fact, there was a fully inflated dinghy on the deck of the trimaran, ready for use but ignored by Houlgrave as he considered it would have been blown away by the wind. James was wearing neither a lifejacket nor a harness as he thought that the weather did not warrant them. The wind was force 4 with a short steep sea of perhaps 6 ft (2 m).

There are many more examples. Just to illustrate how easily and unexpectedly tragedy can occur I will list some cases from my own home waters. There are countless others from all parts of the world.

On a spring day an experienced sailor took his wooden gaff yawl out for a sail on the North Sea coast. It was a fine sunny day with a gentle breeze. He was accompanied on the trip by a colleague from work who had never sailed before. As they turned back for the harbour after two hours, the skipper handed the tiller to his friend and went to the foredeck as the yacht tacked. For some reason or other he lost his balance and fell overboard. He shouted to his colleague to take down the sails. But his friend, suddenly alone in unfamiliar surroundings, panicked, got tangled up in the ropes and fell overboard himself. It was only by luck and great effort that he himself managed to clamber back on to the boat. Eventually he succeeded in starting the engine, but his search for his friend was fruitless and in the end he had to be rescued from the boat in a state of shock and treated in hospital.

Take another example. A 54-year-old yachtsman was drowned when he fell between his boat and the pier in a small picturesque harbour. His was one of three yachts that had arrived there cruising in company. His friends found his body floating in the harbour just after midnight.

Or another example. Fishermen found the body of a man floating in a river. He had been celebrating the night before and apparently fell off his safely moored boat during the night.

In the Alimos marina at Athens a 60-year-old French sailor fell off his boat during the night. His body was only discovered in the harbour the following morning. His wife was asleep and did not notice his disappearance in the night. An autopsy later showed that he had died of heart failure, probably caused by the sudden shock of falling overboard.

• • • • • • •

# Man overboard in the Whitbread Race

*It would have been unthinkable once for a boat to finish a race after losing a man overboard, quite apart from the fact that the rules forbade it. But times, and the rules, have changed and three boats crossed the finishing line in the 1972/73 Round the World Race with one man less than they had set out with.*

From the beginning it was always considered contrary to the spirit of yacht racing to cause avoidable damage to a competing boat or ever, in the quest for victory, to endanger the lives of one's own or another boat's crew. This notion is confirmed by the racing rules which also say, among other things, that a crew member falling overboard has to be picked up again before the yacht may finish the race. That means, of course, that if someone who has fallen overboard cannot be found or has drowned, the yacht has to retire from the race.

The fastest boat in the 1973/74 Whitbread Race over four legs around the world was *Great Britain II*. 'She was skippered by the entrepreneur Chay Blyth, a professional adventurer, whose yacht to the value of £125,000 was built for him by a patriotic millionaire, who would hand the yacht over to Blyth at the end of the race.' This is from the introduction to *The Longest Race* by Peter Cook and Bob Fisher. For me it sheds some light on the attitudes that lie behind the way these races are sailed.

The victim in the case of *Great Britain II* was Bernie Hosking, a 27-year-old paratrooper and one of Blyth's crew of nine. Before his death on the third leg he had already fallen overboard once, but on that occasion was miraculously saved. That was on 11 October in the southern Atlantic.

'It was in the early hours of the morning of 11 October and still dark, when I felt in my bunk that *Great Britain II* was heeling over more than before,' Blyth recalls. 'I got up instantly and saw on my way on deck that a squall had filled the spinnaker, bending the boom dangerously. At once I called all hands. Within seconds the entire crew was up on deck. When the manoeuvre was begun and we eased off the spinnaker, the boom broke and crashed to the deck in two pieces.'

Bernie Hosking, who was on the foredeck to gather the spinnaker, was hit by the flailing sheet and whipped overboard.

'He is in the water!' Blyth shouted.

Blyth continues, 'The next ten minutes were fantastic. Brian threw a light and a danbuoy into the water, but both fell short. Len was at the wheel and I shouted to him to keep an eye on the course and remember it later. Allan was ordered to keep watching the spot where the accident had happened, but it was still pitch black and he couldn't really see anything. Robbie eased off the spinnaker halyard and Mike brought the sail under control. Brian was sent below decks to start the engine and fetch a searchlight. After the sail was stowed, Len gave Alec the course and time run since the accident and Alec converted this into the course to be steered back. The crew were all on deck as we motored back in a slight zigzag. Eddie searched the sea with the light, sweeping it from side to side.

'And then we heard a faint cry from Bernie. The direction from which the cry had come was easy to identify. It was then that I knew we would pick him up again. He was not a good swimmer, but his heavy-weather gear filled with air bubbles would help to keep him afloat for a while.

'We shouted and Bernie answered, and then Eddie had him in the beam of the searchlight. It was awesome and terrifying to see his head bobbing in the dark water, a tiny spot in the beam of light. We threw him a line, he grabbed it, and then many hands hauled him back on deck.

'"Are you all right, Bernie?" I asked him.

'"The water is cold," was his only answer.

'After a mug of hot soup and back in dry clothes, Bernie was nearly restored to his old self again. A few bruises aside, he had not been injured. He was a very happy man.

'The operation to save him had only taken seven minutes, but to us these minutes seemed like an eternity. I think that after this practical demonstration it must have been very clear to every crewman on board that, having fallen overboard, the chance of being picked up again was very slight indeed.'

Most of all, Hosking himself should have been convinced of this fact. Or did he become reckless after this lucky escape?

Be that as it may, during the third leg of the same race, he fell overboard again. This time the yacht was *en route* from Australia to Cape Horn.

'In winds of force 5 to 6 and with six people on deck we had just increased the sail area,' Eric Blunn recalls. 'I was on the aft deck to trim the sheets of the boomed out No 3 genoa. Up forward a sail tier had fouled one of the hanks and Bernie was trying to separate the two. He must have used too much force because when the tier came free he just toppled over the bow into the sea.'

This time it was John Rist who shouted the dreaded 'Man overboard!'

'At that instant, one does not realize the danger inherent in the situation,' Blyth writes. 'But we all knew that this was deadly serious. "Head up!" I shouted, "Head the boat up!" and "All hands!" At the same time I glanced aft, where I could only just see a dark blue bundle in our wake. This was Bernie Hosking.

'In the meantime, the danbuoy and several other emergency devices had been thrown overboard. The foresail was back on deck and the mizen staysail had been taken down. We tried to beat back to the spot where he was in the water, but the reacher hindered us – so that went down too. We now had a westerly wind of force 7 against us, and the men on deck worked hard and fast. Len, our most experienced helmsman, had taken the wheel again and Alec, the navigator, noted courses steered and times elapsed.

'It was just like during the first man overboard manoeuvre; the best people had taken up all the key positions. We now searched a triangle, which we sailed around twice, before we tacked to and fro, listening hard. But we only heard the sound of the sea around us, no reassuring cry from him this time, and we never saw his head bobbing in the water either.'

The minutes passed but time was against the crew of *Great Britain II*. The water had a temperature of 39°F (4°C) and it was quite unrealistic to believe that anybody could survive more than an hour in these icy waters. The clock ticked on while *Great Britain II* twice found her danbuoy in the sea, confirming at least that they were searching the right area.

After two hours they realized that Hosking must be dead, but nonetheless the search went on. Eventually all hopes had to be abandoned. 'Bernie, of all the crew members, distinguished himself by the fact that he had a natural instinct for sailing,' Chay Blyth later said. 'And this made him an exceptional seaman. In time, he would surely have become one of the best offshore sailors imaginable.'

From the Southern Ocean Blyth had to transmit the following message: 'Lost crew member Bernie Hosking overboard on 6 January 1974 at 2140 GMT in position 52° S, 174° W. Search has now ended. Please notify the race organizers and his family.'

Every member of the crew wrote a report of the incident, which were all incorporated into the official report after the finish of the leg in Rio de Janeiro. All their statements have one thing in common: they make it clear that a very simple, one might even say insignificant, event led to this tragedy. It is another reminder that often the most trifling things cause accidents and deaths.

Soon after the search was abandoned, *Great Britain II* resumed her course due east under full sail once more. She rounded Cape Horn on 23 January and was first across the finishing line at Rio on 7 February.

'Of course the crew were shocked by Bernie's death,' Blyth said. 'Bernie was our friend. But his death is something that we all know we have to live with, so we had to accept the facts and continue the race. My crew consisted mainly of paratroopers, for whom the idea of death is not strange. All are active soldiers, and some had indeed experienced the deaths of some of their comrades in combat. This tragic death therefore would not have caused such a shock to them as it would perhaps have done to a civilian.' And that's that. The race, it is argued, has to continue.

It also continued for two other yachts, each of which had lost a man. On 20 November on the second leg from Cape Town to Sydney, Paul Waterhouse fell overboard from the Italian Swan 55 *Tauranga*. The Italian boat had a crew of 11, of whom Paul Waterhouse was the only Englishman. That day the boat was running before a strong to gale force wind under main and twin headsails, sometimes surfing down the waves at great speed.

It proved to be a dangerous ride. As Waterhouse came on deck the yacht broached. One headsail backed, the spinnaker boom with which the other was boomed out broke free of the mast track, became twisted around the sail and threatened to tear out the clew.

Waterhouse crawled forward on deck to clear the sail and take down the remains of the boom in order to prevent further damage. As the yacht was brought back on to her original downwind course, the backed jib suddenly filled again with a loud crack and Waterhouse was catapulted high in the air by the sheet as it came taut. He first hit the deck and then fell into the water.

Immediately all sails were lowered on *Tauranga* and the rest of the crew searched for him for nearly four hours under engine, but of course with diminishing hopes of success. In these high latitudes and the mountainous seas it would have been a miracle to have found him alive. Very probably he was already unconscious after hitting the deck (he made no attempt to grab one of the lifelines) and equally probably he drowned immediately after falling into the sea.

Even though the sad news was soon made known to all other competitors in the fleet and the race committee took the opportunity to seriously remind all competitors to use extreme caution while working on deck, the next man drowned only three days later.

This time it was the turn of Dominique Guillet, one of the two skippers of *33 Export*, a 57 ft (17.37 m) aluminium yacht with a crew of seven. The yacht's position on 23 November was about 45°S, 81°E, in winds of force 9 to 10 and heavy seas, when the two skippers decided to change down from working jib to storm jib. During this sail change, in which two other crew were involved, the yacht suddenly rolled far over to starboard. In the black night co-skipper Millet was just able to grab the shrouds of the mizzen mast and hold on while the three others were washed off the deck. Two of them managed to stay with the yacht, but Guillet did not.

It was particularly tragic as he was wearing a well-proven type of harness at the time. All three men had attached their harnesses to the same jackstay. When the three of them were thrown simultaneously into the water by *33 Export*'s sudden heel the stay broke under the strain. Their lines slid down the broken jackstay and off the end.

The accident occurred at night and it took the remaining four crew some time to haul the other two men who were clinging to the boat back on board. Meanwhile the yacht sailed further downwind.

Now the six of them tried to return to the position of the accident, first under sail and then under engine. However, the yacht itself was endangered by the huge seas and after 20 minutes the co-skipper Millet had to take the fateful decision to abandon the very unpromising search in favour of saving the yacht. In the cold water Guillet would not have survived much longer than ten minutes anyhow.

Thus the 1973/74 Whitbread was the first offshore race in which yachts continued to race after men had been lost over-board and drowned. Since then there have been several other tragic incidents on long ocean races, which again were not reflected in the outcome.

One has to wonder what value is put on human life in these commercially sponsored ocean adventure spectaculars.

• • • • • • •

# Man overboard drill: theory and reality

*There is no shortage of theories about the best way to rescue a man overboard. Doing it in practice can be a different matter, as the crews of the following yachts almost found out to their cost.*

On any sailing course the students are obliged to learn and practise at least one man overboard manoeuvre. But these routines are seldom even remotely similar to what happens in real life. Gerd Wildeshaus is one of the many who, having successfully completed a sailing course, came to realize this: 'By the time I completed the practical test for my sailing licence I could, amongst other things, bring the boat up next to a floating lifejacket in nearly flat calm conditions. One day in the Adriatic Sea I realized how useless this was.

'In a force 2 and seas of less than 1 ft (30 cm) the ensign staff fell out of its fitting at the stern. After three man overboard manoeuvres conducted in textbook manner, we still hadn't retrieved it. On impulse my wife jumped overboard to put an end to the problem. She thought it would be easy to swim over to the staff and back to the boat next time around and climb on board via the bathing ladder at the stern.

'The reality proved to be different. Whenever I was on the right course to pick up my wife, from her point of view low down in the water it seemed as if I was going to run her down so she quickly swam away. On the other hand, the boat never stopped long enough for her to be able to swim up to the bathing ladder. Even though she was not hindered by a lifejacket and is a good swimmer, she could not keep up with the boat once it started drifting to leeward. After three unsuccessful attempts to pick her up I threw her a lifejacket attached to a long line with which I was eventually able to pull her back on board.'

Some countries, in fact, specify in their safety regulations

24

that yachts should have a lifebuoy on a 30 m (33 yards) float-ing line on board. The reasoning behind this is as follows.

If someone goes overboard the crew throw him a lifebuoy without a line to help him stay afloat. In heavy seas it is far too dangerous to manoeuvre a yacht close to a person in the water, so the yacht sails in circles around the victim towing the other lifebuoy on the end of the floating line. It should not take long for the person to grab hold of the line at some point. This method has several advantages, one of them being that the person in the water does not have to try to swim to the yacht and expend energy and warmth in the course of what may prove to be several unsuccessful attempts.

A floating line like this could have helped the crew of *Young Alert* who lost a woman crew member overboard in the English Channel in the summer of 1984. Her skipper too discovered that man overboard drill is very different in theory and in practice.

'When we sail for pleasure I always try to be as relaxed as possible,' he says, 'so I will not always insist on lifejackets being worn or harnesses attached as long as it does not seem necessary. At dusk around 2000 we were roughly 12 miles off the Isle of Wight and making good speed. The decks were dry and none of us were wearing lifejackets as I thought it unnecessary.'

The wind was south-west force 5 as the 6 ton gaff cutter sailed on into the gathering night through a lumpy sea, with a crew of five including three women. Harnesses would have been appropriate for the deck watch at least. They paid the penalty when they were struck by a freak-wave:

'Tim held on to the forestay and I jumped into the shrouds. From here I could see the boat engulfed in a mass of water and pinned down on her beam ends. Then a startled cry ... and Joan was washed out of the cockpit.'

Tim threw a lifebuoy which failed to reach her. The skipper tacked *Young Alert* and started the engine. The other women lowered the foresails. 'Then we tried to reach Joan by coming up to her from the leeward. But it was hopeless. The cutter pitched wildly and the propeller kept coming out of the water. We had to keep up speed in order to be able to manoeuvre. We threw Joan a line, but she had no strength left to hold on to it.'

In desperation the skipper launched the half-inflated dinghy off the coachroof and jumped into it. This, of course, was itself a dangerous undertaking, as we saw in the *Hamrah* tragedy.

'I had the feeling that the dinghy was drifting downwind faster than I could row back. I could only see Joan when we both happened to be on the crests of waves. I was dependent on the crew for information to enable me to find her in the darkness. When I finally reached her she was very weak but still conscious.'

After tacking again, Tim and the others brought the cutter up to the dinghy and threw them a line. They managed to pull the boat alongside and lift Joan aboard.

What lessons are to be learnt from this near-catastrophe? The skipper of *Young Alert* mentions these:

- It may be impossible to bring a yacht alongside someone in the water.
- The most a fully clothed person can do in the water is try to stay afloat.
- A successful rescue depends on luck. We were very lucky but it was still a dreadful experience.

Normally a yacht can still reach port if one of the crew is lost. But with two-person crews, typically a husband and wife, the situation is much more critical if some misfortune befalls the skipper, in which case the remaining person needs to be able to sail the yacht on his or her own. And this can happen despite all safety precautions; one skipper had a heart attack while he was up the mast checking something in the rigging, just before the yacht arrived in Barbados after a hitherto successful Atlantic crossing.

Another yacht to lose half her crew was a Trintella ketch sailing from Papeete, Tahiti, to San Diego, California. Nine hundred miles from the Californian coast the ketch was hit by hurricane Raymond with winds of 110 knots and waves as high as houses. The boat capsized and lost not only both of her masts but also the skipper who had been secured in the cockpit by his harness. His wife was below decks harnessed to the saloon table and suffered a head injury. She was unconscious

*The two photos on this page and the one on page 28 show various tactics used to recover a casualty overboard. This photo: Throwing a floating line, with a buoyant object on the end, to a man overboard.*

*If the casualty cannot reach the line it can be drawn towards him.*

*Using a tackle attached to a halyard to get the man back on board.*

for an indefinite period, but she then managed to bring the yacht back to Hawaii under a jury-rig in 40 days, with a maximum noon-to-noon run of 60 miles.

The experienced blue water sailor Dierk Cordes conducted trials of safety equipment and procedures on the yacht *Wappen von Bremen* during an Atlantic crossing with some interesting results.

He writes, 'Half-way across the Old world to the New in position 34° 55.5'N, 52° 38.5'W we decided to try our safety procedures. During the trip we had already staged a few fake emergencies which had shown us how careless we really are at sea, despite our good intentions.

'Through these safety trials we achieved a new understanding of the term "safety at sea" and we confirmed that no procedure is as good as not falling overboard in the first place. We do not view safety equipment as useless, but nevertheless one certainly has to keep its value in perspective.

'As well as testing our man overboard drill we wanted to film and photograph the yacht under full sail at sea. So we launched the dinghy in moderate weather with a lazy swell and winds of force 3 to 4. The two people in the dinghy were laden not only with cameras but also with most of our safety equipment – whistle, flares, danbuoy and the like. So while the people in the dinghy were filming us from all angles we were seeing how good the equipment was and from what distance it and the dinghy were visible.

'Our drill went well. As we sailed away from the dinghy one person plotted the courses and distance sailed very accurately so that we could have returned to it virtually blindfold. But of course this demanded not only continuous communication between helmsman and navigator, but also a degree of coolness which in the case of a real emergency one would probably never have.

'The man overboard manoeuvres that we practised made it clear to us that the highest priority of all is to stop the yacht as quickly as possible at all costs, such as even sacrificing sails for example when the boat is running under spinnaker. The greatest danger is that the yacht sails on too far and the person in the water is lost from view. All the textbook manoeuvres taught in sailing schools are utterly useless and even dangerous because most of them require the yacht to be sailed on for quite a distance until the victim is probably out of sight.'

Skipper and crew of *Wappen von Bremen* then went on to record how far the dinghy and other equipment could be seen under nearly ideal conditions, a moderate breeze with only small waves without whitecaps and a long lazy Atlantic swell. The sun was out. Visibility was good. Nevertheless their results are remarkable:

'At a distance of about one cable (200 yards) the dinghy could no longer be seen, but the danbuoy with a flag on a 10 ft (3 m) spar was still visible.'

In other words, a person in the water, whose head is only 4 in (10 cm) above the surface, not 40 in (1 m) as the people in the dinghy, is lost from view much sooner. The dinghy is out of sight within 60 seconds even in perfect conditions. Someone in the water will probably be out of sight after 20 seconds. This may seem like plenty of time, but at sea it is nothing. Within the space of less than half a minute the accident has to be noted, rescue drill set in motion and the boat stopped or even turned around on its way back to the victim.

'At three cables the danbuoy was nearly impossible to see,' Cordes continues, 'but the orange smoke from a hand-held flare was easily spotted.'

This is at a distance of 600 yards (550 m) and illustrates how important it is to mark the position of the accident instantly with a danbuoy even if it falls short of the person in the water.

'At four cables the danbuoy vanished from sight, but we could clearly see a small hand flare being fired. However, we thought that the flash was too short and we think it improbable that a ship passing by chance and not specifically looking out for it, would have noticed it.

'At seven cables we could clearly see the white star fired from a signal pistol, which stayed above the horizon for a while, but even then one should remember that no ship at sea will have a lookout constantly scanning the horizon.'

All these observations were made by people on the yacht who were specifically looking out for the dinghy. The rest of the crew, busy with working the sheets and sails, did not notice any of this.

'The two people in the dinghy lost sight of the yacht very quickly and only glimpsed it when both boats were on wave crests at the same time.' Cordes ends his report by repeating the elementary rule, 'The only real life insurance is to stay on board. Safety depends not so much on sophisticated safety equipment but on a very healthy fear of falling overboard!'

And on using adequate safety harnesses on deck. The lines should be at least four-strand 12 mm nylon rope and the jackstays at least 8 mm wire. Attention should of course also be paid to the terminals of the wire and their anchorages. Finally, as the tragic accident on *33 Export* shows, not more than one crew, or at most two, should attach their harnesses to the same jackstay.

# 2
# GROUNDING

## *Total loss*

*Yachts that run aground do so mainly through navigational errors. For* Helene III *it was a case of wandering off course.* Crystal Catfish *was steered to disaster by her self-steering gear.* Song *was caught among dangerous reefs in darkness.* Northern Light *lacked the basic navigational equipment which might have saved her. The owners of three of these yachts then lost to looters the little that they had not lost to the sea.*

The experienced blue water sailor Gerd Bücking lost his tried and trusted Nicholson sloop *Helene III* on 28 December 1983 in the Galapagos Islands. The German dentist had already competed in the 1976 OSTAR in the boat and had now sailed from Gran Canaria via West Africa and Cape Horn to the Pacific archipelago.

During a night passage with Bücking and one crew on board, *Helene III* veered off course and ran aground off the island of Santa Cruz. The small cruiser, from which only a few things could be saved, soon became a total loss. Even in these remote islands looters were at the site of the stranding only hours after the incident and removed any items of value from the wreck.

It is not surprising that at sea singlehanded sailors place so much trust in their self-steering gear. These proven robot helmsmen are sophisticated and reliable. Most of them steer a more accurate course than any human helmsman could. Their drawback is, of course, that they steer in relation to the wind. If that changes, the yacht too will change its course. Approaching the coast and especially half a dozen hours before the landfall, the skipper or a crew should therefore, if not steer by hand, at least keep watch and a good lookout.

The American singlehanded yachtsman John J Hunt entered the 44 ft (13.4 m) sloop *Crystal Catfish* in the interesting Bermuda One-Two Race of 1977. Starting in Newport, Rhode Island, the competitors had to sail to Bermuda singlehanded, then back with a crew on board.

On 25 June at around 0200 he was north-east of Bermuda on the first leg of the race and according to his dead reckoning about 20 miles off. Two radio bearings of the beacons at Gibbs

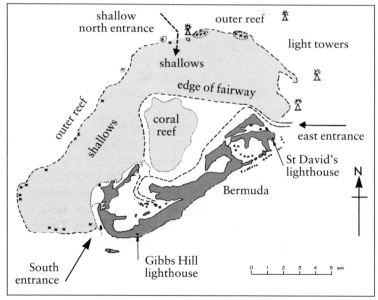

*Approaching from the north-east, the owner of* Crystal Catfish *thought she was on course to pass safely east of Bermuda, but instead she struck the outer reef to the north.*

Hill and Kindley taken at different times remained unchanged. So Hunt assumed that he was running parallel to the eastern side of the islands and that he could stay on the same course. Nearing the end of the 650 mile passage he retired to his berth to be fit for the landfall at dawn. Only minutes later the wooden sloop with 59 ft (18 m) tall mast ran aground.

'At first it was only a little scraping below the keel, which had me jumping to my feet in an instant,' Hunt recalls, 'but even before I could put on my harness the scraping developed into a splintering noise, like an arm breaking. It was horrific! "God, we have collided with a ship," was my first thought as I rushed on deck. And indeed, the high steel structure close beside the boat looked just like the bridge of a ship. But it was not moving and just stood there in the water.' What is it?

As Hunt disentangled his harness from the sheets there was another crunch, much louder and more alarming.

'It's a lighthouse. It looks like a lighthouse,' Hunt thinks, 'but how did it get here? And why is it not lit? Where am I?' Then, the full realization dawned on him: 'It's the reef! I have managed to hit one of the beacons marking the northern end of the extensive Bermuda shoals.'

He went at once to his VHF set and transmitted a distress call: 'MAYDAY, MAYDAY. This is Whisky Echo 3902, *Crystal Catfish* calling Bermuda Radio. I have run aground on the reef directly next to a lighthouse. Over.'

He then returned on deck to try and save the situation. But there is nothing he could do. Meanwhile he missed Bermuda Radio answering his distress call and requesting a clearer position: 'Is it the St David's light at the east tip of the island?'

Below deck once more but unaware of the coast station's request, he transmitted a second distress call, now near to panic: 'MAYDAY, MAYDAY, MAYDAY. This is *Crystal Catfish*. I am aground on a reef next to a lighthouse. The boat is badly damaged and sinking. Over.'

Again he did not wait for a reply. Some minutes later as the yacht is going down he sent off a third distress call, but still with the vague position 'next to a lighthouse'. Then there was no time to wait for a reply. He boarded his inflatable dinghy and the yacht sank on to the rocks about 16 ft (5 m) below the surface.

A few minutes later he was picked up by the ketch *Minstrel*. Before he boarded that boat he retrieved his EPIRB, avoiding a long search by the coastguard. *Minstrel* informed the coast radio station that she had the shipwrecked yachtsman.

The series of errors which led to the grounding and subsequent loss of the yacht could have been avoided. If Hunt had kept at least a partial lookout he would possibly have seen the large 50 ft (15 m) high beacon rising above the clearly visible top of the reef in time to change course. His fix, relying on two radio bearings, was wrong because only a few days previously the authorities had moved one radio beacon, Kindley, close to the other on Gibbs Hill. But despite this unfortunate circumstance, the entire responsibility still rests with the skipper of a boat and he alone bears the blame.

Another important lesson to be learnt from the loss of this yacht is that when a distress call is transmitted one should wait for a reply and be prepared to answer simple questions, as to the position of the yacht for instance.

Bermuda Radio tried to contact Hunt to find out more details, but at the time he was busy on deck. In desperation the radio station finally ordered a lifeboat to the St David's lighthouse, which was where they assumed the incident to have taken place. But, in fact, this was at the opposite end of the island and miles away from *Crystal Catfish*.

Many yachts cross the Atlantic each year and their number is increasing. Each of them faces the problem of making a safe landfall on the other side of the ocean. Most offshore yachtsmen use celestial navigation and obtain accurate positions with a sextant. Some of them are apt to forget that, as land approaches, coastal navigation begins again with its different demands and practices. Particularly in the days before GPS, some would steer straight for port on the basis of their most recent celestial observation, without regard for time of day, state of tide, sea conditions or visibility. Two eminently avoidable strandings, one on each side of the Atlantic, serve to illustrate the point.

The small cruiser *Song* was lost on the reefs of the Vieques Sound in the Caribbean Sea. The owner, George Harrod-Eagles, had sailed the small bilge-keeler, which was fitted with

34

an 8 hp auxiliary engine, singlehanded from England to the Canaries and then on to the Caribbean in the summer of 1981. He was attempting a circumnavigation.

On 14 January 1982 *Song* left Martinique bound straight for Fajardo on the east coast of Puerto Rico. The sailing conditions at this time of year are ideal, but *Song* had some difficulty pointing high enough against the north-east trades to reach the partly buoyed channel between Isla Vieques and Puerto Rico. On the afternoon of 18 January *Song* was about 20 miles away from Fajardo. To reach harbour the boat would have to head first north-east, then north. The trade wind was light and the current would be against *Song* in a few hours, so the engine had to be used.

'It was a difficult decision,' the singlehanded sailor later recalled, 'but one in which I should have borne in mind the golden rule of navigating in reef-encumbered waters – never sail at night! There were three options and I was anxious to reach port before the darkness.

'(1) Should I look for an anchorage for the night? This seemed rather ambitious considering the unsettled weather, lack of information on the holding ground and the disastrous

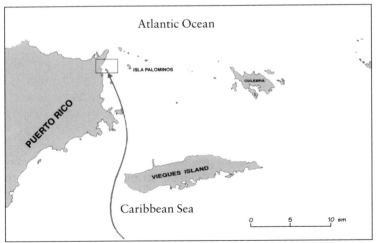

*Song's course from Martinique took her through the Vieques Sound and up the east coast of Puerto Rico towards Fajardo (see map on page 37).*

consequences if the anchor dragged at night.

'(2) Should I turn around, sail back to the open sea south of the islands and heave-to until the following morning? I could not bear to think of this for it would have meant losing all the ground to windward that I had gained so slowly and painfully over the past hours.

'(3) Should I just hold my course to the north? Any why not? The sun still shone warm over the sparkling sea and the scene looked just like an advertisement for the Caribbean. There were some unmarked channels between islands and reefs, about one or two miles wide. A mile by day is quite a comfortable distance. At night it suddenly shrinks to a dangerously narrow gap, but I did not think of that at the time. I had come to a decision and so I sailed on towards my destination.'

It was a fatal decision. The tide which had now turned slowed *Song*'s progress under motor and the small cruiser was still ten miles from harbour, when dusk fell and the silhouettes of the small islands and rocks became more and more indistinct. Soon the few dimly lit buoys could no longer be seen against the backdrop of bright lights on the coast, so *Song* had to be navigated with the help of some lights already passed and now astern. It was too late to turn back now.

'I took down all sail and was on the lookout for white water,' Harrod-Eagles remembers. 'The echo sounder showed ten metres [33 ft]. The bright lights of the houses on Isleta Marina, on the far side and partly obscured, were to port. So I had already passed the southern reef and had only one more, the northern fringe of another reef, ahead of me. The sounder jumped to five metres, then seven. I went below to fetch the chart and fix a position from these soundings, but suddenly the echo sounder showed two metres and the next moment we ran aground.

'The keel bumped over the rocks maybe half a dozen times, then *Song* was hard aground on a coral reef. The realization that this could be the end of my boat and my voyage was terrible. All the measures I took to try and free her were taken in a hurry and semi-panic, from trying to trim her fore-and-aft by running up and down the deck to wiggling the rudder or pushing and poking with the boathook.'

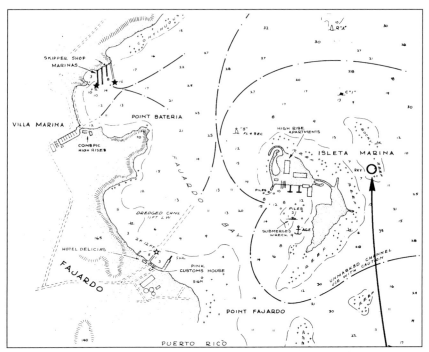

Song *ran on to a reef north-west of Isleta Marina. The bright lights on the island made navigation difficult as* Song *was skirting it on her way into Fajardo Bay.*

Breaking seas quickly pushed the boat further and further on to the reef and lifted the boat and crashed it down again on to the coral once every five seconds with fatal consequences for the hull. Harrod-Eagles had to accept that his boat would not survive the night. So he transmitted a distress call on VHF and was rescued a few hours later by the local coastguard.

On his return in the shoal-draft coastguard vessel the following morning to try and save at least some of his personal belongings, he faced a shocking discovery. Looters, about whom the coastguard had warned him when he was abandoning the boat the previous night, had already been at the scene in the early hours. Boom and mainsail, genoa and working jib, spare sails, anchors, warps, fenders and navigation lights were gone from above decks. Below decks clothes and books were missing, as was the camera, radio, kitchen utensils and the stove. Only gaping holes remained where not long before the SSB and VHF radios had been mounted.

'The worst for me was the loss of my log book and my sextant,' he says. 'I had become used to the possibility of losing my boat and maybe even my life to the sea. But having to see how *Song* had been looted ... I would have preferred to have her sink in deep water, maybe through a mistake of mine, but at least without those thieving hands on her.'

*Northern Light* was also looted after grounding on the Spanish coast on 10 September 1982. Ann and James Griffin were experienced blue water sailors. They had owned their sturdy, 45 ft (13.7 m) wooden gaff cutter for 22 years and had already crossed the Atlantic four times in her. On passage from America again, they arrived off the Strait of Gibraltar on the night of 9/10 September. Since the end of August they had experienced continuous bad weather with strong winds and poor visibility. For the past couple of days they had been unable to shoot the sun for a fix, nor was there any chance of seeing Cape St Vincent, the south-western tip of Europe.

The 62-year-old couple had bought an electric self-steering device in Bermuda, but the investment did not pay off. After only one day at sea the device failed and the couple had to steer by hand all the way across the Atlantic. *Northern Light*'s equipment was rather modest, with only a sextant, log, a dozen flares and a fibreglass dinghy. They carried no liferaft, no electronic navigational instruments, no radio and no echo sounder.

'It was so hazy that we had had no sight of land in the past two days,' Ann Griffin records. 'But the log was reliable and we reckoned to have half a knot of favourable current under us towards the Strait of Gibraltar. This was confirmed by the pilot book. Just after sunset we could see a ship and during the night a further 21 vessels passed us, all steaming east. We must have been near to the strait.

'The following morning was again hazy and we could neither see land nor obtain an astronomical fix. At noon we were suddenly in green water with a fishing boat less than a mile away. The chart showed us where we were (on the Trafalgar

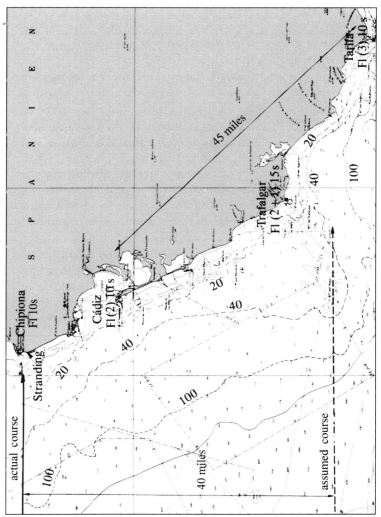

*Attempting to make a landfall near the Strait of Gibraltar without an echo sounder,* Northern Light *ran on to rocks off the Spanish coast near Chipiona. The DR was out by 40 miles after her Atlantic crossing and the crew mistook the Fl(2)10s light at Cádiz for the Fl(3)10s light at Tarifa, 45 miles away. The chart also shows the 100 metre depth contour which they could have followed to the Strait if they had had an echo sounder.*

Bank), but the coast only eight miles away was still invisible.

'During the afternoon the wind veered from south-east to west and at around 1930 we could see a light, flashing group 3, every ten seconds. This could only be Tarifa. We celebrated with tea in the happy anticipation of being in Gibraltar by morning.

'But then we noticed the number of lights ashore. Too many for Tarifa, which we had passed nine years ago. Could the town have changed so much in that time? We became suspicious, started the engine and changed course.

'But it was too late. Seconds later we hit a rock and then grounded. The rudder had broken on the first heavy impact, then the propeller jammed. We managed to stem the water flowing into the boat for the first three hours, pumping every five seconds, while we fired all our flares and shone our searchlight at every car passing ashore. Finally, the water rose above the floorboards and triumphed over the pump.'

Ann Griffin's report ends like all the others – sad, defeated and still incapable of grasping the whole truth of what had happened. 'I could not believe it. From time to time we had touched a coral reef in the Caribbean, but had always managed to get free by ourselves. But those reefs were soft compared to the one that now held us in its grip. We had to abandon *Northern Light* before she heeled over too much and crushed the dinghy beneath her. Jimmy rowed two miles towards the coast and then a two further miles along the breakers before we could find a beach. How we managed to cross the surf and reach the beach safely, I don't know.

'Where were we? In a military area south of the Guadalquivir estuary. The light we had seen was not Tarifa, but Cádiz, also flashing every ten seconds, but group 2.'

It took five days for the military authorities to grant the owners permission to return to their yacht and attempt salvage. But she was by then beyond help. Looters had already removed all the deck gear, leaving only the interior equipment in place, which was under water and probably unserviceable anyway.

This stranding could have been avoided with the aid of an echo sounder, a basic piece of kit for any boat, both for making a landfall like this and for navigating in inshore waters.

Coming in from the Atlantic depth contours could have

been clearly identified with an echo sounder, first 100 metres, then 40, then 20. This would have enabled the Griffins to check their dead reckoning. Around the Trafalgar Bank the 100 metre contour describes a 90 degree bend towards the Strait of Gibraltar. They could have followed the contour at a safe distance from the shore and this point would have been noticed even under the prevailing conditions with poor visibility. The stranding of *Northern Light* happened, after all, 40 miles north of the Trafalgar Bank and nearly 50 miles northwest of Tarifa. An error as large as this is not expected when the characteristics of lights are allotted, although it is of course undesirable to have nearly identical characteristics for two lights on a long stretch of featureless coast.

● ● ● ● ● ● ●

# End of a classic yacht

*The loss of a large yacht shortly after leaving harbour in light winds may seem hard to credit. But what began as a seemingly minor setback developed slowly but surely into a disaster.*

The 40 ft (12 m) yawl *Gravita* built in England in 1906 was not a new vessel, but she had been beautifully restored. She was now on her way to the Caribbean with a crew of six. A reconditioned Mercedes Benz diesel had just been fitted in Cádiz and now in October 1986 she was on her way south. She sailed down the African coast, following the route inshore of the Canary Islands.

The inshore route obviously offers the possibility of calling at ports *en route* and visiting foreign towns. About half-way to the Canary Islands *Gravita* stopped for two days in the little Moroccan fishing harbour of Al Yadida. The voyage so far had been plain sailing. *Gravita* was, after all, sailed by an experienced crew, with a skipper and a mate who were both well qualified for sailing these waters.

After two days in harbour *Gravita* left Al Yadida on a Sunday night at 2230. There was no detailed chart for the bay of Al Yadida on board, but as they had previously entered the harbour (by day) with the help of sketches from other cruising boats the skipper felt quite confident.

The chart showed the two powerful breakwater lights of the harbour, but the reef that extends from Cape Mazagar roughly one nautical mile to seaward was not marked. But the chart did show a wreck symbol on the shallow reef with depths of less than one metre, not far from the spot where the

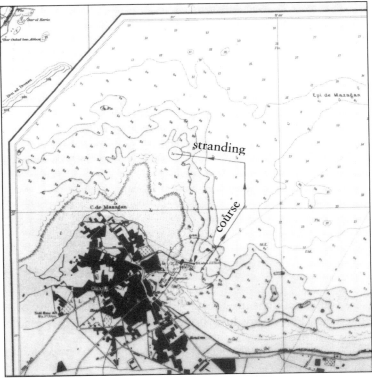

*Chart showing the port of Al Yadida, Morocco, and the course of* Gravita *before and after her engine failed to where she eventually grounded.*

graceful *Gravita* was lost. It happened in the following way.

*2220 hours* *Gravita* leaves harbour under engine. Visibility is good. After passing the breakwaters a NNE course is steered for ten minutes, then a northerly course for another twenty minutes. During their stay in port the crew have observed the reef and its position, so they believe that they can find their way safely across the bay even at night. The moon is about half full and only a little help.

*2250* Suddenly the engine stops. This takes the crew by surprise as it has just been fitted and was believed to be in good condition. But all attempts to re-start are fruitless.

*2255* The skipper decides to hoist main and genoa while two crew members try to find the engine fault. *Gravita* gathers little or no way and pays off on starboard tack.

*2305* The keel touches bottom for the first time. The boat is able to go about, but the keel keeps hitting rocks and she makes little or no headway.

*2310* The skipper decides to lower all sail and to anchor. At anchor *Gravita*'s bow swings round to the north-east, facing the onshore swell.

*2320* The anchor starts to drag. The crew fires five red distress flares. Wind and swell drive the boat further towards the shore, bumping over the reef.

*2330* The skipper fears that the rudder is damaged and that the yacht is making water. Due to the darkness, this is hard to verify. The crew are now in a state of panic, caught off their guard by the sudden and totally unexpected turn of events.

*2335* The yacht is filling rapidly. The bunk cushions are afloat as the crew gather their passports, ship's papers and money in preparation to leave the yacht.

*2340* *Gravita* is now resting on the rocks at an angle of 45 degrees. There seems little hope of saving her. Further distress flares are fired.

*2345* The inflatable dinghy is launched. The outboard, which has got wet, will not start. Two crew members paddle off towards the harbour.

*0030* The two reach the harbour, leave the dinghy at the yacht club and report the stranding to the police and customs. The latter alert the civil rescue service.

*0100 Gravita* is by now full of water. The bridge deck is submerged. The crew abandon their attempts at pumping and baling.

*0130* The angle of heel increases alarmingly, becoming dangerous for those on board. Seas break over the yacht. The liferaft is inflated and made fast alongside.

*0200* A boat of the civil rescue service arrives on the scene and takes off two crew members in the inflatable.

*0300* An attempt to drag *Gravita* off the rocks by a local fishing boat and the rescue service inflatable is unsuccessful. It is still dark and operations near the rocks are quite dangerous. Further salvage attempts are postponed until the next high water in daytime. The skipper and the last crew member leave the yacht.

*1030* The crew return to the scene with the local fire brigade to assess the chances of salvage.

*1230* At low water the full extent of the damage becomes clear. The yacht is a total loss. Parts of the planking are gone. Rocks protrude into the yacht's interior. All the joinery is destroyed. Coachroof and forehatch are gone. *Gravita*'s crew give up all hope of salvage and await the insurance company's surveyor.

*Next day, 1000* The surveyor arrives from Casablanca. With the still shaken crew he goes out to the wreck. During the past 20 hours looters have been on the boat and removed the engine. The bridgedeck around the winches has been cut in half for easier access to the equipment inside. Anything of value has been dismantled and taken away at intervals.

The abandoned wreck of a yacht legally belongs to no one. It is the responsibility of the local authorities and it is up to them whether to tolerate or to prosecute looters, who often appear on the scene of any wrecking within hours. To defend the yacht from them, the crew of *Gravita* would have had to stand by the wreck in the dinghy or liferaft. Only then could they have protected their property against looters and preserved their claim to salvage.

The only piece now remaining is the five ton lead keel. As it would cost more than it is worth to salvage the keel, it still lies in shallow waters on the reef as a memorial to this fine yacht.

A disaster like this might seem to be virtually impossible – a seaworthy yacht, ready to cross the Atlantic, full of sophisticated navigation equipment, lost just one mile from harbour on a calm clear night. Were the crew's minds already thousands of miles ahead, in the Caribbean?

• • • • • • •

# The wrong light

*In the course of a voyage round the world the yacht* Christine II *ran ashore while attempting to make harbour in Aruba in the Lesser Antilles. The mistake: trying to enter a tricky, unfamiliar, and poorly lit harbour at night. The good news: there's a salvage company at the port and the insurers pay up promptly.*

*Christine II* with the Suhr family on board had already been in the Windward Islands for a considerable time. Now, she was about to leave Marigot Bay, St Lucia, for Curaçao, 500 miles downwind in the trades. *Christine II* left Marigot Bay at 1800 – timing which contributed to the disaster at the end of the passage. In the trade winds steady noon-to-noon runs of 120 miles might have been assumed (or an average of 5 knots for the 41 ft (12.5 m) yacht), meaning that she would arrive more or less exactly four days later. It would thus have been wiser to leave Marigot at a time of day suitable for the intended landfall and approach to Curaçao. Leaving in the evening, with darkness approaching, was committing oneself to a landfall in the hours of darkness.

The experienced offshore yachtsman Gerald Edlinger said: 'I always try to up-anchor at such a time that I am bound to reach my destination just before dawn. Then the lights will help me to confirm my position and I will have a full day in which to negotiate potentially complicated harbour entrances.'

'We had an easy passage,' recalls skipper Lothar Suhr. 'We reached Willemstad on 13 June at 1620. The wind was about force 6. As we were about to enter we saw a small sailing boat being thrown about by the waves in the outer harbour, waiting for the swing bridge which bars the way into the sheltered inner harbour to open. The yacht was apparently having great difficulties in keeping clear of the pier and not being smashed to pieces. The bridge did not open. It was a testament to the experience and luck of the other boat's crew that they eventually managed to clear the harbour and get out again. It was then that we decided to carry on to Aruba.'

It must be remarked at this point that although a bridge clearly is an obstacle for yachts, this one was a well-known one. It is mentioned in the pilots of the area where it is also said that yachts sometimes have to wait a long time for it to open as the island's main road traffic flows across the bridge. Again, it would have been better if *Christine*'s skipper had planned to arrive off Willemstad in the morning, and not at the end of the day.

In the event, *Christine II* had to sail on into the night. 'With an easterly wind, about force 6, and good sailing conditions we reached the south-eastern end of Aruba at 2100,' Suhr states. 'We were now standing off the long reef, very very tired after the long and rough passage. We sailed along the south-west coast of Aruba to Oranjestad and sighted many lights, but with characteristics which we did not recognize. As we later learnt, the lights of Aruba had been changed just three months previously. The coast was easy enough to identify, but navigation was very confusing. After passing the large industrial harbour of Barcadera we thought that we had identified the entrance. But we sailed on to Oranjestad and tried to find the entrance there.'

The pilot says that of the three harbours that lie behind the long reef off Aruba only Oranjestad is suitable for yachts. Barcadera and San Nicolas are major ports for the oil industry. So far, *Christine II* had made the right choice.

'The harbour of Oranjestad was easy to make out, the reef not,' he continues. 'It only reaches above the surface in a few spots and is overgrown with mangroves. Most of it is about half a metre below water. Up until now we had entered many harbours at night and felt confident of our abilities. But here we just could not identify the lights of the channel through the reef to Oranjestad and so we motored the couple of miles back against wind and current to the industrial harbour of Barcadera. Clouds obscured the full moon. It was raining lightly. The engine was running smoothly and the seas were about one metre.'

Was it due to fatigue that the Suhrs could not find the well-lit channel to Oranjestad? Now they were on their way back to Barcadera and soon they could see the ships moored alongside the piers behind the low reef. A quiet night in harbour seemed to be within their grasp.

'A white light outside the reef marks the entrance. There are more white and green lights behind the reef, but their positions in relation to each other are difficult to make out from the sea. I turn to port in the firm belief that there is at least another 100 metres to the reef.'

But Suhr is mistaken. Christine is the first to spot the reef – white water directly in front of the bow. Her cry, 'The reef is just ahead of us!' cannot prevent the inevitable. At her warning, Suhr goes full astern, but at that moment, the cruiser's keel touches bottom. Will the engine be able to pull the yacht back into deep water? A large wave rolls out of the darkness and effortlessly lifts the 14 ton yacht on to the reef. More waves follow and *Christine II* eventually settles down on the rocks about 10 metres from the outer edge of the reef. That the yacht does not become a total loss is due only to her strong construction.

Roughly once every five seconds the boat is lifted and dropped down again on to the coral. She settles on her port side and starts to fill with water. A third of the keel and the bilges aft are severely damaged. Some of the ballast is pushed upwards under the engine.

'We fire red distress rockets and contact port control on VHF,' Suhr continues. 'They acknowledge our distress call and immediately send a pilot boat out to us. But even though it has only a very shallow draft it cannot reach us on the reef. One of the pilots jumps into the water and swims over to us with a line. We launch our dinghy and eventually reach the pilot boat through the surf. The bottom of the dinghy is ripped open on the coral, but we hold on to the line and reach the boat safely.'

So the Suhrs leave their stricken vessel. When they are brought ashore with their five-year-old son long after midnight a tiring process of formalities begins. But how could the boat have stranded just 100 yards (100 m) from the wide and well-marked channel?

Suhr recalls, 'As already mentioned, a white light marks the entrance to starboard. We had a white light on our starboard side, but it was behind the reef. In theory it should have been impossible to see it from seaward, but the plate that obscures the light in that direction had dropped off ages ago. So we mistook the light for the entrance light, the latter being hidden from us by the mangroves.'

It took three more boats (two Venezuelan fishing boats and a large American yacht) to hit the reef, before the missing plate to obscure the light was finally replaced and the mangroves covering the entrance light were cut down.

The Suhrs had a stroke of luck in their desperate situation. There was a Dutch salvage company in Barcadera which they contacted immediately after being put ashore the same night. In the morning, Christine and Lothar Suhr returned to their stranded yacht which lay over at an angle of 45° on the reef. The man from the salvage company announced, 'The boat will have to be lightened and she will probably sink when we pull her off the reef.' The Suhrs were appalled, but the man continued, 'But we have just what's required: three huge rubber floats, each capable of lifting ten tons. They should do the job. We will attach them to your boat and start salvaging her today, before she is battered to pieces. Before then you must try and take off as much heavy equipment as you can.'

The company provided large plastic bags in which the most valuable and heaviest equipment was ferried ashore across the lagoon. It was hard and painful work among the sharp coral, waist-deep in water, and inside the listing boat. Load after load was ferried ashore by dinghy, where everything was thrown into a large container without much care or ceremony.

The anchor landed on top of the bag with the electronics. The wet blankets were thrown on top. Eventually everything was ashore and the salvage men said that they would try and float the yacht off the following morning.

The meeting in their office, with tea and cakes, was friendly and relaxed, until the men got down to business. 'We can only start when we have eight thousand dollars on the table, here,' they said, still smiling but determined.

They also smiled at Lothar Suhr's response: 'You can't do that, you will have the vessel and container full of equipment as security!' But they all knew that the yacht was worthless until it was off the reef and that the equipment in the container was probably ruined.

'Eight thousand dollars and we start work,' the men insisted. Suhr had not got the money. His insurance company in Germany would have to pay.

Here Suhr was again lucky; he was insured with a highly efficient, helpful company. What is the use of a low insurance premium when it comes to the crunch in a foreign port, with the yacht being battered to pieces on the reef? In this situation even hours can make the difference between salvage and total loss.

Two faxes were sent from Aruba to Hamburg, one to the insurer, the other to Suhr's bank. Thirty minutes later the bank faxed back: 'The money is on its way.' And the insurance company replied within the hour: 'Carry on with the salvage. Price to be negotiated by the Lloyd's agent in Curaçao.' This second fax was worth £50,000 to the Suhrs. The insurance brokers in Hamburg, all of them keen sailors themselves, had taken the decision as swiftly as possible and thus helped to save the yacht.

The next day the salvage began. The floats were fastened to the outside of the yacht. The seas had gone down since the previous day and the large modern tug with its 3,500 hp engine could reach the wreck from the outside of the reef. Still, it proved to be difficult and dangerous to attach the towline to the yacht and only in the afternoon could the tow commence. The master of the tug was cool and professional. For ten minutes or more the mighty propeller of the tug churned the water, but the yacht did not move. The captain was being careful. He could have increased the power and dragged her off; instead he just kept up the strain on the towline and waited. He was waiting for a larger than average wave. After ten minutes they could see one approaching, longer and higher than those before. It reached the yacht, lifted her, and she was afloat.

She floated for one minute, then for another, but then she slowly started to sink. A large pump was shipped across in the tug's dinghy. One man disappeared into the cabin in an effort to stem the leak with cushions. But the hole was too big. At the last moment the salvage team saved themselves and their pump before the deck and coachroof disappeared below the waves. However, she did not sink completely as the floats kept her partially afloat, even though half-submerged. Very very slowly she was towed towards the harbour mouth. Here there was another delay, caused by the harbour authorities. They wanted to make sure that she would not sink in the entrance and ordered the tow to wait for a while to prove that the yacht could remain in her half-floating, half-submerged state.

At last they were allowed in and an hour later the yacht was craned out of the water and put ashore. Over the next few months, thanks to the enthusiasm and energy of her crew and money from the insurance claim, *Christine II* was transformed from a wreck into a sea-going yacht again. In the autumn she was relaunched and sailed off through the Panama Canal into the Pacific. Happily for the Suhr family, the reef off Aruba did not prove to be the end of their circumnavigation.

• • • • • • •

# A rude awakening

*The Belgian blue water yachtsman Patrick van God and his wife Wendy, after rounding Cape Horn in their yacht* Trismus, *struck a reef in the Tuamotu Islands while they slept. They survived the disaster on this particular occasion.*

Patrick van God rounded Cape Horn on 22 May 1972 from east to west at the age of 31. His yacht *Trismus* was a sister ship to Bernard Moitessier's *Joshua*, a steel double-ender with a length of 39 ft (12 m) and a displacement of 14 tons. The Belgian had given up his profession as a dentist and with his wife was now on his way to the Tuamotus, after extensive cruising in Chilean waters and a visit to the Galapagos Islands.

The islands of the Tuamotu group are difficult to approach. They are only a couple of feet above sea level and, despite the palm trees on them, can only be seen from a few miles off. By day the outer coral reefs can be easily identified by the seas breaking on them, but on a dark tropical night, even one with a full moon, it can be nearly impossible to spot them early enough.

Van God (whose full surname is van Godsenhoven) left Papeete with his wife Wendy on 24 March 1974, bound for the Tuamotus. According to their celestial navigation they were 38 miles away from Rangiroa at 1600. Due to very light winds they were only making 2 knots and thus reckoned not to make a landfall before 0700. Van God also assumed a west-going current which might delay it even longer.

As the tropical night descended at 1800, the experienced sailor and his wife retired to their berths and left the boat to sail on alone with the vane steering gear. As usual, the alarm clock was set to go off two hours later, so that one of them could go on deck for a look around.

Around midnight van God was on deck for a look. The sea was calm. There was next to no wind and the boat was consequently making less than 2 knots. In the black night he could not see anything that would hint at land being nearby. He returned to bed and *Trismus* sailed on.

According to his dead reckoning the reef should have been 20 miles away at this point. For a crew that had sailed for 15 days since the last port it was only a short distance. Certain questions naturally arise. How reliable was the last fix? How far should one rely on dead reckoning taking current into account? How reliable is the log? Is 20 miles an adequate safety margin for a fix by celestial navigation and dead reckoning with at least another six hours of darkness to come?

Van God described what happened next: 'At 0156 I was thrown out of the bunk by a terrible shock. I dashed outside. We had struck a reef! I turn the wheel and let the boat bear off on port tack, but *Trismus* only hits the reef again. Wendy starts the engine. "We will make it," I try to convince myself. But the next moment the engine stops and *Trismus* drifts back on to the coral. The alarm clock goes off below just as a huge breaker lifts the boat high on to the reef.'

Shipwrecked in the middle of nowhere! The skipper was haunted by the question of how it could have happened. Was the log wrong? Or the sextant fix? How could *Trismus* have covered 38 miles in ten hours in so little wind?

At noon next day a sun sight revealed that *Trismus* had struck the extreme southernmost point of Rangiroa's coral reef. Had she pointed just a little higher for the past four days she would have cleared it easily. As van God looked back at his dead reckoning it becomes clear that, while he reckoned on a west-going current, the set was actually due east.

For 12 long days the van Gods tried to get *Trismus* back into deep water, but they could not move her even a yard. The sea destroyed the uninsured yacht that was high and dry at low water and covered by the breakers at high water. Eventually they had to give up and leave the wreck.

Van God drew this lesson from his shipwreck: 'One should always use the pilot published by the local authorities in each area.' In this part of French Polynesia it would have been the French *Instructions Nautiques* that actually record the east-setting current. The English pilot, on the other hand, contains an erroneous record of a west-going stream.

Gipsy Moth V *was wrecked under the lighthouse on Gabor Island, 250 miles from Sydney, during a singlehanded race while her skipper slept.*

'Our last chance to clear the reef was missed when our engine failed. The reason for this was tragically simple: the safety line which we always tow at sea fouled the propeller as we motored astern.' Van God adds another observation: 'In future I will never take such a risk when approaching an unlit coast at night. No matter what the weather may be like, I will always heave-to at a distance of at least 30 miles and wait for daylight.' Perhaps he might have added: 'And when there are two people on board, one will be on watch throughout the night, no matter whether we are sailing or heaved-to.'

He continued, 'The fate of *Trismus* was a lesson in humility. As sailors, we always believed we did not make mistakes and we would never experience shipwreck if we did not make mistakes. But it was a mistake that led to this loss. The life of an ocean sailor that we have chosen is full of risk and adventure. But the uncertainty is one of the strongest attractions for me. If you relinquish the security of urban life you must be prepared to lose all your possessions without warning in one sudden disaster.'

Three years later van God lost not only his yacht, but also his life. Competing in the Mini Transat from Penzance via the Canary Islands to Barbados, he vanished without trace. Somewhere at sea a ship may have run him down while he was sleeping. Everyone has to sleep sometime, and singlehanded sailors are very vulnerable when they do.

While another singlehanded skipper slept – in this case Desmond Hampton – Sir Francis Chichester's former *Gipsy Moth V* ran ashore during a race. Just 250 miles from the finish of the second leg of a round the world race at Sydney, the yacht struck the rocks of Gabor Island. The self-steering gear was steering the yacht while Hampton slept and she changed course because of a windshift. Hampton was saved but *Gipsy Moth V* was a total loss.

• • • • • • •

# Too much faith in technology

*At the moment when the large charter yacht*
Orion X *struck the Great Barrier Reef the*
*skipper thought it was 55 miles away. How*
*much faith should you put in electronic*
*navigators? How far should you check your*
*position by other methods?*

*Orion X* was a wooden cruising yacht, 65 ft (19.8 m) long,
built in 1927. She had a 132 hp engine and a radar with a
range of 24 miles. Her owner and skipper, Günther Lohse,
used her as a charter boat. On 15 November 1982 he left
Cairns in Australia at around 1730 bound for the Torres Strait
and Sri Lanka.

At midnight on 16 November *Orion X* passed the narrow
Trinity Opening, checking her position by visual bearings of
lights. As the yacht headed out to sea the Walker 402 satellite
navigator was switched on. Lohse had bought it in Sydney. On
the way to Cairns it had worked well.

One can hardly blame Lohse, on the second day at sea and
out of sight of land or any navigational aids, for relying on the
satellite navigator instead of using celestial navigation. The
red control lights on the Walker had registered several satellite
fixes during the day and it would have worked these fixes into
its own dead reckoning. However, it might have seemed odd
that the positions given by the navigator drifted further and
further away to the north of the skipper's own DR. Lohse put
it down to a current of 3 knots, mentioned in the pilot for this
time of year.

The skipper, who had taken the first night watch with
another crew member, had no chance to alter course when the
yacht, sailing fast on a broad reach, suddenly crashed head-on
into a reef that lay directly in her way at 2245. The long-keeled
yacht was driven so far up the reef that she could not get off,
either under engine or sail.

At low water, about three hours later, she capsized to port, planks splintering on the impact with the rocks. Lohse had his charter party taken off by an Australian motor cruiser. A few hours later his vessel was a total loss.

A court later had to decide the question of why the satellite navigator at the time of the stranding had shown a position of 14°02.76'S and 145°43.51'E when the actual position proved to be 14°56'S and 145°45'E or about 55 miles further south.

Of course it is easy to point out that Lohse should not have relied on the satellite navigator alone. But, on the other hand, why should one buy such an expensive and sophisticated piece of equipment if not to relieve some of the burden of navigation? Günther Lohse had previously sailed on merchant ships for several years, latterly as first mate on a cargo ship. He was a professional navigator, accustomed to coastal and celestial navigation, accustomed to interpreting the information in pilots and on charts about currents and tidal streams.

It is interesting to note that the court did not blame him for being overly reliant on the instrument, but it concluded that he had in fact made mistakes when using and programming it. In that case at least part of the blame perhaps should rest with the manufacturers of the Walker 402 for not making it more foolproof.

On the trip from Sydney to Cairns it had worked perfectly. It thus appears that it was not faulty. What had caused the instrument to show the wrong position on the yacht's last voyage could only be guessed at. Various possible explanations were put forward, such as the following.

(1) The instrument was programmed incorrectly before setting off, for example by entering the wrong time. (According to the manual, however, the instrument would not have been able to recognize satellites if the difference between entered time and actual time was more than 15 minutes.)

(2) The tidal data entered was incorrect. This error would have caused a significant error in the position given by the instrument. According to the manual, variations along the north–south axis have the gravest consequences.

(3) The fact that the red light was on was not an indication that the instrument had actually been able to convert the satel-

lite signals into fixes. This type of satellite navigator is, above all, an automatic DR calculator that shows a DR position based on the data on the display until this is verified or corrected by a satellite fix, but the red light only indicated that the instrument had received the signal from a passing satellite, not that it had actually converted it into a fix. (This was explained in the manual.)

(4) A satisfactory satellite fix depends on several factors, such as a satellite zenith of between 10° and 75°, a time error of less than 15 minutes and an actual position that is no more than 60 miles away from the DR position.

The court came to the conclusion that, as there had actually been nine usable satellite passes on the day of the stranding, the instrument had for some reason not been able to convert them into fixes. And it continued by stating that the skipper, Günther Lohse, should have used conventional navigation to check the position given by the instrument. For not doing so he was found guilty of negligence. The court made a significant distinction in not finding him guilty of gross negligence, in which case the insurance would not have been obliged to pay.

Commenting on the case and its decision, the court made it clear that had Lohse been first mate of a merchant ship he would have been found guilty of gross negligence. He would have been expected to check the ship's position by all methods at his disposal and not trust in one system alone. But as the skipper of a yacht, this yardstick could, in the court's opinion, not be applied. It was acknowledged that he had not acted out of carelessness or laziness, but had simply trusted an expensive and sophisticated piece of equipment. Furthermore, he had been able to explain the difference between the DR and satellite positions in terms of the north-going current mentioned in the pilot.

The maritime court in Flensburg in this judgment of 19 December 1983, therefore, made a distinction between a navigator on a ship and on a charter boat.

• • • • • • •

# The dangers of speeding

*The spectacular end of a fast motor cruiser that
ran ashore in a well-marked estuary was more
like a road accident than a shipwreck. The boat
was travelling so fast that it ran right up the
bank before capsizing at the top.*

On Saturday 3 April 1982 two friends, Rolf Rehbein and Julius
Homann, took the fast 30 ft (9 m) motor cruiser *Medusa* for a
trip on the river from Travemünde in Germany. They called at
a night club in Lübeck and had a few drinks with two young
ladies whom they subsequently invited back to the boat.

Rolf and Julius and the two girls decided to visit another bar
in Timmendorf, about 19 miles away. Rolf was an experienced skipper while Julius had never helmed a boat along a
river at night. It was unfortunate, therefore, that Rolf decided
to leave Julius at the wheel while he went below to show one of
the girls round the boat. It was also unfortunate that at this
point the river developed serpentine qualities, requiring quite
a drastic change of course on the part of the helmsman. Also at
this point in the river, the line of lit buoys ended. Needless to
say, as the river curved to starboard the boat didn't; instead it
ploughed straight up the stony bank doing 25 knots!

The impact must have been tremendous for those on board;
the boat, weighing 3½ tons, slid 70 ft (21 m) along the bank
before finally coming to rest on its starboard side – but not
before it had catapulted Julius and one of the girls into the
water. Once all four people had made their way ashore, the
girls promptly ran off leaving the men to hitch-hike to the
nearest town to report the accident.

In the subsequent court case, the two men tried to claim that
an oncoming boat had forced them up on to the bank, but the
court saw through this with the aid of statements from the two
girls and found Julius and Rolf guilty of gross negligence.
However, by employing a clever lawyer, they succeeded in
having the original verdict overturned.

● ● ● ● ● ●

# The three shipwrecks of
# Bernard Moitessier

*The great singlehanded sailor Bernard
Moitessier was shipwrecked three times between
1952 and 1982. On each occasion he was
devastated by the loss but recovered to resume
his seafaring existence with a new vessel.*

The legendary ocean wanderer Bernard Moitessier who traded
certain victory in the first singlehanded race around the world
for a life of cruising the Pacific lost three yachts through shipwreck.

Moitessier lost *Marie Thérèse* on a September night in 1952
off Diego Garcia, the most southerly of the Chagos Islands, in
the Indian Ocean while he was on passage from Singapore to
the Seychelles. The boat was 'a wonderful junk from Singapore, smelling of natural oils' with whose simple but powerful
lines Moitessier had instantly fallen in love. But his navigational equipment on this first of his blue water cruises was far
from comprehensive.

'All I had', recalls Moitessier, 'was a compass and a sextant,
barely enough to obtain a noon latitude. For the past two
months, I had always relied on guessed longitude as I had no
chronometer on board. Nor did I have a log or a radio with
which to receive the time signals that could have transformed
my old alarm clock into a chronometer in order to obtain
longitude. That would probably have been accurate enough to
reach the Seychelles and sail around the Chagos bank that lay
between *Marie Thérèse* and her destination.'

As Moitessier lacked these basic navigational instruments
he relied upon his seafaring instinct, hoping that he could
'smell' land and detect it by various signs, like clouds on the
horizon, floating seaweed, an abundance of flying fish, the
changing rhythm of the swell and finally sea birds, certain
species of which never venture further than 40 miles out to sea.

This rather romantic notion might not seem to be accurate enough for offshore sailing. On 4 September his DR position put him 500 or even 600 miles east of Diego Garcia, but his instinct at the same time warned him to keep his eyes open. 'But I could detect no sure sign of land', he recalls, 'and the sea displayed the totally impassive poker face that it always assumes when it does not want to give away any of its secrets. But the warning stayed within me, although I could not see anything unusual.'

Before sunset, the singlehanded sailor scanned the horizon particularly carefully, but again nothing was to be seen – no birds, no seaweed, no clouds. He went to his bunk and came back on deck an hour later. He corrected the course, then hesitated. Should he change it a few more degrees or leave the helm lashed as it was? Then he retired to his bunk again to sleep.

'The moon had just begun its descent towards the west when a sudden sharp jolt threw me against the starboard side of the cabin,' he continues. 'In the next instant I was on deck, clutching the mizen mast to avoid being swept off by the huge wall of water that smashed over the boat with all the fury of a sea breaking on the shore. *Marie Thérèse* leaned over on her side as the seas broke over the reef, which was covered by less than one metre [40 in] of water. There she lay, only half a cable's length away from Diego Garcia. There was a faint smell of mangled coral and loose algae. Then a third sea broke over the hull with terrible strength. A pitiful groaning sound came from her timbers as the corals to which *Marie Thérèse* was pinned bit deep into her. "In this chaos of white spume", I thought, "the death of my vessel will be swift."'

It was swift. When the new day dawned *Marie Thérèse* was dead. The keel was gone, ribs and planks smashed. 'And I cried for my memories, for my books and a lost world without limits into which I had grown so completely that I could not imagine any other world. But above all I cried for my lovely boat.'

*Marie Thérèse II*, 27 ft 5 in (8.36 m) long with a beam of 10 ft 4 in (3.14 m), was built a few months later on Mauritius using local labour and timber. The yacht, again 'the most beautiful vessel on earth', had a draft of 5 ft (1.5 m), a long keel and a ketch rig. Alas, this boat had only a short while to live. *Marie Thérèse II* sailed from Mauritius to the Caribbean where she in turn was wrecked off the rocky north-west coast of St Vincent on 8 April 1958, again at night, again as her skipper slept.

Moitessier had sailed from Trinidad to Martinique to slip *Marie Thérèse II* and give her a new coat of antifouling. After the work was finished he planned to return to Trinidad as quickly as possible. During the work on the boat and during the first part of the passage back he had little or no rest.

'When night came the wind freshened to 3 or 4 Beaufort from the east,' Moitessier recounts. 'On the northern tip of the next island, St Vincent, there was no light. So a third night without sleep approached. Nothing serious. But despite the warmth of the tropical night I was shivering through and through. I had not eaten properly for a few days. At ten in the evening the sky became overcast. All night one rainy squall followed the next. The night was as black as ink. I drank coffee and yet more coffee in an attempt to beat fatigue. Why had I not included some stimulants in my first aid kit?'

When he could stay awake no longer, he trimmed the sails and the self-steering gear and set his alarm clock to wake him up in half an hour. How sweet would sleep be now!

He continued to sleep for half an hour at a time and at 0100 there was still nothing in sight. But the night was so utterly black that it would have been impossible to see anything anyway.

'It was nearly two o'clock when a severe jolt awoke me,' he recalls of his second stranding. 'I jumped on deck, disengaged the self-steering and tried to gybe. I had set the alarm for half-past-one; it must have gone off already. Then a second shock jarred the boat, followed immediately by a third and accompanied by the groaning of tortured timbers. *Marie Thérèse II* was perched on top of a rock, while the seas broke over her deck and cabin. The rudder had been wrenched from the boat. It was dangling in the sea still attached by the steering cables. All this happened in only a few seconds.'

Moitessier clung to the mainmast and threw the anchor overboard, which was normally stowed at its foot. But too late.

'It is the end. As before, I escaped without physical harm:

bad weed never dies. But for my innocent boat the bell tolled. I could only cling stupidly to the mast, embracing my love for the last time, the most beautiful boat on earth.'

Moitessier's third shipwreck happened 24 years later, with his boat *Joshua* that had become famous in the meantime. The plans for this steel ketch were drawn in Trinidad immediately after the loss of *Marie Thérèse II*. The 39 ft 7 in (12.07 m) yacht with a beam of 12 ft 1 in (3.68 m) had a hull thickness of 12 mm (0.47 in) at the keel, and 7 mm (0.28 in) and 5 mm (0.2 in) at the underside of the hull and the topsides. This heavy boat displaced 13½ tons. The mast and rigging, carrying 1,076 sq ft (100m²) of sail, were also unusually strong.

*Joshua* made some remarkable long-distance passages. Between the years 1963 and 1966 she was sailed from Marseilles through the Panama Canal to the Pacific and via Cape Horn back to France. In 1966 Moitessier was awarded the Blue Water Medal. Then came the most famous chapter in his career, beginning with the singlehanded round the world race of 1968/69 and culminating, after two crossings of the Pacific, in Tahiti.

He remained in the Pacific after 1970, making it his home. He visited countless anchorages in French Polynesia and along the west coast of America, often sailing with his wife and friends. In 1982 he sailed from San Francisco for the Mexican anchorage of Cabo San Lucas, on the southern tip of Baja California, with the actor Klaus Kinski.

Twelve days after leaving San Francisco *Joshua* arrived in the broad sandy bay on 3 December. There were around 100 other boats in the popular anchorage, many of them anchored with a long line led ashore. This method of mooring saves a lot of room as the boats cannot swing and stay in one place. On the other hand they have less chance of escape in a sudden onshore gale, hemmed in by their neighbours and secured both to an anchor, and to the shore. The bay is open to the east, but nobody was worried; the hurricane season with winds from this sector was long past.

On 6 December there was no weather forecast, as there was a fault with the satellite. Moitessier did not like the look of the weather and put a second anchor, a heavy CQR with chain

1–2 *The tug* Aito *drags the steel yacht* Yin & Yang *off a coral reef in the remote Tuamotu archipelago. Even though the yacht was insured, the owners ended up with nothing.*

3–4   *The last resting place of the charter yacht* Kensho *which was driven ashore by a typhoon while at anchor in the Philippines. The owner married*

5–6   The 30 ft (9 m) steel yacht Andijk stranded on the German island of
Juist in the North Sea during a force 10 north-westerly in September 1985.
Her crew of three escaped unharmed. At low tide, heavy machinery was
br ught in to dig the       ht out of th  sand and remove her by land

7–8 *The 39 ft (12 m) fibreglass yacht* Venus V *went ashore on the coast of Brazil near Rio de Janeiro because of steering failure and losing her anchor, after crossing the Atlantic from the Gambia in 1985. The largely undamaged*

9

10

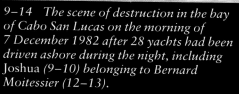

9–14 The scene of destruction in the bay
of Cabo San Lucas on the morning of
7 December 1982 after 28 yachts had been
driven ashore during the night, including
Joshua (9–10) belonging to Bernard
Moitessier (12–13).

15

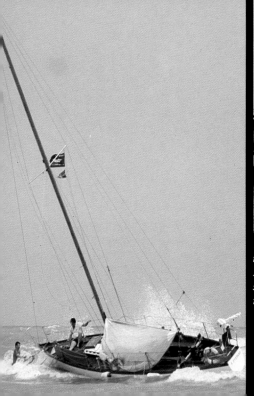

15–17 *A classic Italian yacht which was driven ashore in the Adriatic during a short-lived summer gale. She was later refloated with the aid of a crane.*

and warp, ready for instant use on the foredeck. And then, taking everyone by surprise, the wind swung around to the east.

Moitessier again: 'At sunset, it blew from the south-east, the wind increasing. I am glad I had the second anchor on deck, as I felt a premonition. As the wind increased further during the night, a high swell ran into the bay. Suddenly my heavy CQR broke out from the sand. Immediately I dropped the second anchor that was on deck, and *Joshua* turned her nose to the wind once more. But then an extremely heavy squall hit us and it did not seem to abate. *Joshua* dragged again, increasingly quickly. Soon she hit the beach and was turned broadside-on to the swell, seas breaking over her. My mind simply refused to comprehend the awful, horrible truth.'

Moitessier sent his crew to safety ashore, remaining on board himself. Inside the heavy steel hull he was not yet in danger. But the boat was thrown about by the breakers and he had to wedge himself on the floor.

He had time to reflect: 'I could now clearly see the things that I did not want to see before. I saw the clouds building up. In Joshua Slocum's day there were no weather satellites. The seaman had to keep his eyes open. I looked, but without seeing. The satellite was out of operation, but there were still clear signs in the sky. Moreover I anchored too close inshore and too close to the other boats. So I had no room to manoeuvre when I still had the time to reach the open sea. All I could do was to squat on the floor boards like a stupid ape and do nothing but think.'

Then something happened which Moitessier in his steel boat had not reckoned on. The 46 ft (14 m) yacht *Freling* was driven on to the beach next to *Joshua* and started crashing against her previously undamaged hull. But worse was to come. The other boat's rigging got entangled in *Joshua*'s and what the sea had so far failed to do was now done by the boats themselves; they destroyed each other. Both were dismasted as they collided. Lengths of aluminium mast and *Joshua*'s wooden topmast came crashing down. The tangle of broken rigging on deck almost blocked the companionway and Moitessier was lucky to reach dry land.

Sunrise found 26 stranded yachts on the beach. At low water Moitessier clambered inside *Joshua*, which was little more than a hulk. Below decks was unimaginable chaos. Water poured in through the broken portholes. The hull was full of sand and the debris of her equipment. 'My boat is a wreck and so am I' is Moitessier's bitter summing up on 7 December.

But there were helpful people on shore and several younger sailors who did not want to see the famous *Joshua* ending her days like that. Fifty pairs of hands, assisted by mechanical diggers, freed her from beneath *Freling*. They cleared out the sand and debris and somehow managed to drag the heavy steel ketch back into the water. As she finally lay afloat once more, secured by three anchors, Moitessier was surprised to see that the hull was still completely sound without a single leak. Nevertheless he did not want the huge task and cost of turning this floating hulk back into a sea-going yacht. He sold her on the spot and decided to build a new steel boat, smaller, more easily handled, and cheaper than *Joshua*. It took a group of young enthusiasts a year to restore *Joshua* to a seaworthy state, including a completely new rig. In the summer of 1984 she was back sailing once more.

• • • • • • •

# A fateful decision

*On New Year's Eve 1980 the 54 ft (16.45 m)
yacht* Alpha *left Ibiza bound for Genoa with a
crew of three. The weather was far from perfect
but they were in a hurry to get home. They never
got there.* Alpha *was wrecked on the coast of
Sardinia five days later. What became of her
crew is a mystery.*

Florian Zeh is ill at ease as he telephones home to his wife Anja
from the exclusive Ibiza Yacht Club on 29 December. The
wind is howling in the rigging of moored yachts. The
anemometer is reading 30 to 40 knots. But he has a problem;
the insurance on his yacht *Alpha* expires on 5 January and by
then the boat is supposed to be back in Genoa, 500 miles away
as the crow flies. The weather has kept them in Ibiza for far too
long already and time is now running out. His wife tries to
persuade him to wait for the weather to improve or take the
long way round, along the coast via Barcelona, Toulon and
Nice. The distance is not much longer, but Zeh fears that his
crew, Antonio and Mario, will want to spend the cold nights in
harbour if one is close at hand. He is an experienced yachtsman
who has been round the world and across the Atlantic in the
past. *Alpha* is a fine wooden yacht built in Italy, 54 ft (16.54 m)
long with a beam of 13 ft 5 in (4.08 m), draft of 6 ft 11 in (2.1 m)
and 25 ton displacement. She is cutter-rigged with a 100 hp
auxiliary. She really belongs to his wife – Zeh is just the skipper
– but he is determined to save about £1,500 on the premium by
reaching Genoa before the old insurance policy expires.

At 0730 on 31 December *Alpha* leaves Ibiza. The forecast is
giving force 5 to 6 north-easterlies for the Golfe du Lion and
north-east-to-east 7 to 8 for the Balearics. On 4 January Anja
Zeh is waiting for the yacht in Genoa. There are gales in the
Mediterranean but she is not unduly worried. Perhaps they are
sheltering in harbour or hove-to until the weather improves.

In fact the yacht is still afloat, but it seems her crew may

have already perished. On 4 January at 0845 a Signor
Calderini is driving along the south-west coast of Sardinia
and, by chance, observes a yacht lying with her bow or stern to

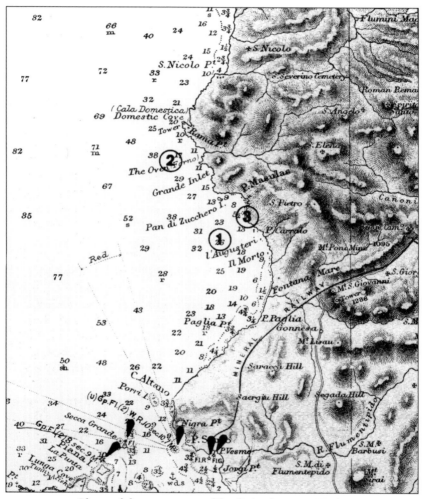

*Chart of the west coast of Sardinia showing (1) the
reported position of* Alpha *at 0845 and 1500 on 4 January,
(2) the reported position at 1700, (3) the position of the
wreck on 5 January.*

the strong winds close to the shore. At 0930 on the same morning a Signora Ponti looks out of her window and spots a quite large round object like a buoy, drifting in from the sea. The sea is very rough that day with a strong wind. Later the same day a Signor Corticelli driving home at 1500 along the coast sees the yacht. 'The hull was a light colour', he recalls, 'and I thought the yacht was stationary, with the bow towards the sea. As I was driving I could not look more closely.'

Finally a Signor Ratti taking a walk along the beach at 1700 observes something. 'About 2 km from where I was, I saw the mast of a boat which I could not make out due to the distance and the generally stormy conditions. I stayed in the area for an hour and the mast remained in the same position. As it grew dark no lights were switched on. So I came to the conclusion that nobody was on board.'

Finally on the next day, 5 January, the wreck is spotted by a Signor Gianoli on the rocks at Porto Masulas. He informs the authorities who identify the wreck, already broken into several pieces, as the yacht *Alpha*. A search is started for the missing crew, but in the course of the next couple of days nothing is found.

On 12 January Anja Zeh contacted her insurance company to claim for the total loss of *Alpha*. The company declined to settle her claim for two reasons. Firstly, they assumed that the yacht had been wrecked after 1200 on 5 January and thus after the insurance had expired. Secondly, they were of the opinion that Florian Zeh had acted with gross negligence, in which case the insurance company would be free from their obligation to settle the claim.

As to the first point, it was soon established that the stranding had, in fact, taken place before noon on the 5th. While the yacht had only been spotted by Gianoli four hours later, there was so much wreckage lying around on the beach that it was clear that the boat must have been there for well over four hours.

The second point is of more significance and interest. The court had to decide whether winter sailing in the Mediterranean is indeed negligent or not. As it happened, one of the three judges was a keen yachtsman, very experienced especially in Mediterranean waters and chairman of the offshore committee of a well-known yacht club. The judges found that sailing in that part of the Mediterranean in December and January does not of itself constitute negligence, which meant the insurers had to pay.

While it is not surprising that yachtsmen take the side of their fellow yachtsmen, especially against an impersonal corporate opponent such as a large insurance company, I feel the court's decision is open to question. In a case like this the

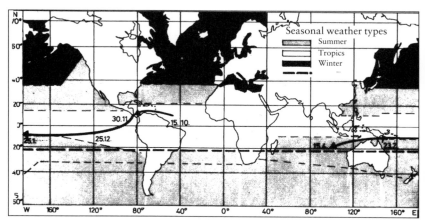

*Seasonal weather types for shipping for the period*
*16 October to 15 April. The Mediterranean is shown as*
*having winter weather (black) at this time.*

court has to define the boundary between what is officially regarded as safe responsible seamanship and what is regarded as irresponsible negligence. If risky passages like that of the *Alpha* are officially approved, then other, maybe less experienced, skippers might be guided into following Zeh's example. For this reason I would query the court's decision and raise the question of whether it is safe and responsible to undertake passages such as this in the Mediterranean in winter.

In my opinion sailing is a sport for the summer. Voyages to the far north, such as to Greenland or Spitsbergen, in the summer are quite safe, as are those to the extreme south, for example around Cape Horn in the southern summer. Both are undertaken in the relatively favourable weather of summer, as opposed to the more dangerous weather conditions of winter.

The map on page 68 shows the different types of weather prevailing in seas around the world in the period between 16 October and 15 April. Conditions in the Mediterranean are classed as 'winter', suggesting that the area cannot be regarded as a safe cruising ground at this time.

It is risky at the best of times to start a passage of 500 miles when the general weather pattern is dominated by deep depressions and the forecast for the day of departure speaks of headwinds of force 7 or 8. Bearing in mind that, in this case, the entire passage might be a beat to windward in strong winds and low temperatures, I do in fact regard the decision to leave port as gross negligence.

The wind chill factor, which was disregarded by the court, probably also contributed to the loss of the yacht and her crew. At the time of *Alpha*'s departure the air temperature was 54°F (12°C) and next day 45°F (7°C). Combined with head-winds of force 7 or 8, the apparent temperature on board would have been between 25°F (−4°C) and 19°F (−7°C).

Furthermore, the weather conditions quickly deteriorated in the days that followed. On the day of departure the Balearics had winds of force 7, the neighbouring Golfe du Lion force 8. The depression that caused these winds was moving south-eastwards and would have brought gales to the area west of Corsica and Sardinia by 4 January. This development may not have been foreseen on *Alpha*, perhaps due to the lack of a suitable radio.

It would have added only 10 per cent to the passage to have chosen the route along the coast, where harbours of refuge would have been available within a short distance of each other.

But the most serious indictment of the whole enterprise must surely be the fact that the boat was seriously under-manned, taking into consideration her size, the length of the passage and the time of year. *Alpha* had no means of self-steering so there had to be someone on the helm at all times. With a crew of three this would mean about 12 hours' work a day for everyone on board, if one takes into account other tasks like navigation, sail changes, cooking and other tasks. And the burden gets much worse if one person is incapacitated by illness, accident or anything else.

So when Florian Zeh decided to leave Ibiza for Genoa on 31 December he was embarking upon a trip of about a week, with temperatures around freezing point, beating into a strong or gale force headwind, roughly 60 per cent of the time in darkness. Personally I would call the decision gross negligence and a contravention of the rules of good seamanship.

• • • • • • •

## Unsafe havens

*More yachts have perhaps been lost in the apparent safety of anchorages than at sea. The proximity of land can represent danger as well as protection and few anchorages offer a guarantee of safety in a tropical cyclone. Often more than one yacht is involved and in Cabo San Lucas more than 20 were wrecked in one night, their numbers contributing to their difficulties.*

It seems obvious enough; as long as there is land to windward, the wind does not change direction and the water is no deeper than 30 ft (10 m), an anchorage ought to be safe. But squalls coming down from high mountains or cliffs, or the presence of land too close to leeward, can put a different complexion on the matter. And if the wind suddenly shifts or a swell runs into the anchorage, a safe haven can soon turn into a trap.

In June 1985 German yacht *Eisbär II* and the Italian schooner *Nova Idea* were anchored in a bay on the north coast of the Greek island of Othonoi when a southerly wind, as sometimes happens when a depression passes, veered rapidly to the north-west and piped up to force 7. Within moments the coast that had previously sheltered the yachts became a lee shore and as the yachts swung to their anchors the rocks became uncomfortably close.

The skipper of the Dufour 31 *Eisbär II* was alone on board at that time but he managed to clear the bay under sail and engine, although he had to sacrifice his ground tackle, a heavy CQR with 150 ft (45 m) of chain. The 72 ft (22 m) *Nova Idea* with 13 people on board was less fortunate. They tried to lay out a second anchor and keep the yacht off the shore with the engine, but the attempt failed in the darkness and with the panic on board. The schooner drifted ashore and was a total loss within minutes. The people on board were lucky to escape with their lives.

Hein Mastmeyer had a similar misfortune. His 33 ft (10 m) yacht *Arcona* was anchored in Honeymoon Bay on Water Island, south of St Thomas, on 7 November 1984 when a hurricane swept through the Virgin Islands.

'The forecast for that day at 0800 said that no storms or depressions were expected,' Mastmeyer recalls, 'only a small depression which was currently 200 miles south of Puerto Rico would be in our area on the following day. This was my first mistake; I believed the forecast.'

On the evening of the 6th a rising easterly wind and a falling barometer make him suspicious. There is a swell coming in from the west and at midnight one of his mooring lines breaks. Mastmeyer starts the engine and drops a heavy CQR anchor with 40 ft (12 m) of chain and 130 ft (40 m) of warp in a depth of 23 ft (7 m). While manoeuvring under engine, he fouls his propeller in a floating line attached to another buoy. The shock shears the propeller shaft and the propeller slips aft and fouls the rudder. Unsuccessfully he tries to clear the rudder.

In the morning the wind is very strong and is now blowing into the bay which is open to the west. Mastmeyer now deploys his so-called 'hurricane anchor', a 56 lb (25 kg) fisherman with chain and warp. This is tied on to a third anchor. The fisherman has to be secured by a nut and bolt.

'This is when I made my second mistake, which eventually led to the loss of my boat,' Mastmeyer continues. 'Although I knew that all shackles and bolts should be tightened with

71

*Repairs under way to* Arcona *after her stranding. Sadly she was completely destroyed by another storm, before she could be refloated.*

pliers, I only secured the nut of the anchor by hand. I saved myself the one minute that would have been required to crawl back to the cockpit and fetch the pliers.'

As the wind rises to hurricane force in the afternoon the boat touches bottom. The anchors are dragging and Mastmeyer finally cuts the warps so that the boat is carried swiftly ashore by the huge ground swell, rather than being slowly pounded to pieces.

'As we later found out, the bolt of the fisherman anchor had opened itself. And with the hurricane blowing at full strength the heavy CQR alone had no chance.'

After three months of hard work under the tropical sun and without electricity, *Arcona* was nearly ready to go back into the water again when another depression hit the island and the sea pounded her to pieces within six hours.

Jack Bordon was perhaps luckier when his boat *Kensho* was lost in a typhoon in the Philippines in 1984. He was waiting for a charter party in a lagoon when the typhoon struck. The anchors dragged and the boat was blown across a reef and deposited high and dry on the white sandy beach. Bordon made the best of the situation. He built himself a hut not far from the yacht, then married a local girl and finally opened a beach bar on the little island that turned into quite a commercial success. But Bordon has yet to reveal if he is really happy, so close to the point where he lost his yacht in which he had sailed 70,000 miles.

In December 1982 a devastating storm swept the bay of Cabo San Lucas in Mexico with its fine sandy beaches and normally good shelter outside the hurricane season. The destruction of 28 yachts including Moitessier's *Joshua* (see page 62) brought notoriety to the popular anchorage.

The weather that night developed as follows: *1700* Sky dark and threatening. *1800* Wind south-east 10 knots. *1900* Wind south-east 30 knots, waves 5 ft (1.5 m). *2000* Wind 50 to 70 knots, waves 11 ft (3.5 m). *2100* Wind 70 knots, waves 16 to 20 ft (5 to 6 m) breaking over the decks of most boats in the anchorage.

Dick and Angie Connell were lucky. Their 38 ft (11.5 m) cutter *Miracle* survived unscathed. 'With the cockpit awash from the short breaking seas, we started the engine to be ready to avoid other boats. Once in the inky blackness of the night we saw the enormous bowsprit of a schooner a few feet above our heads. Several times our keel touched bottom and in the enormous seas we were rolled from side to side until sometimes the crosstrees touched the water. We had several collisions with other yachts and several times our ground tackle fouled that of other boats.

'At 0300 our engine stopped and we expected the worst. But a minute later the wind suddenly veered and became offshore. There was still nothing we could do but wait. To our enormous relief and surprise we were still afloat at daybreak. The waves were still enormous but now breaking in the opposite direction.'

The beach meanwhile looked like a battle-field. Sails and equipment, dinghies, oars, anchors, warps and other bits and pieces littered the sand for miles. The local Mexicans gave food and warm clothes to the shipwrecked yachtsmen.

According to the Connells, three main facts were to blame

for the mass-stranding: 'First, the boats were anchored in too shallow water. Second, we were too close to each other. And third, we should have up-anchored and sailed out to sea as soon as the change in the weather was apparent. Since Cabo San Lucas we have viewed an anchorage through different eyes.'

The 56 ft (17 m) schooner *White Cloud II* survived the night because Paul and Susan Mitchell anchored in deeper water in a depth of 40 ft (12 m). They were well over 300 yards (275 m) from the shore, lying to two heavy anchors with 200 ft (60 m) of chain and 200 ft of warp. They decided too late to weather the storm at sea and could not get out of the bay. Instead they could only drop a third anchor. They also had their engine running, until the cooling water intake was blocked by some of the floating debris and it stopped. Luckily their three anchors held the boat even without the help of the engine.

This is their breakdown of the fate of yachts in the bay. Two boats survived because they were moored from the start in the small inner ferryboat harbour. Three others escaped un-scathed because they moved to the inner harbour before the storm arrived. Six sailed out to sea under storm canvas during the night. Ten boats survived the storm at anchor. Two boats were towed out of danger. All the rest (more than twenty boats) ended up wrecked on the beach.

The Mitchells draw these conclusions from the experience: 'Most of us tend to believe the forecast too much. We do not want to admit that things can take a turn for the worse. Some crews disregarded the signs of approaching bad weather because they had only just arrived after long passages and were tired and wet. But most of the yachts just could not up-anchor quickly enough because they had lines ashore and were lying far too close to each other. Of 12 boats trying to escape this trap only 6 succeeded, and they only by sacrificing their ground tackle. The others got warps and lines around their propellers and ended up more helpless than before.

'Eighteen of the yachts that were wrecked had anchored inside what became the line of breakers during the storm, roughly the 5 fathom (10 m) line. Of the ten yachts that sur-vived at anchor eight were outside and only two inside the line of breakers. It was the force of the steep breaking seas that broke the anchors out. Heavy reliable ground tackle is a help, but that on its own is no guarantee of survival.'

After this experience the Mitchells decided to use only those anchorages in future that can be evacuated under sail if necessary, to double their already substantial amount of ground tackle so that even if some has to be abandoned there is still some left on board, and finally to keep a very sharp weather eye open in any anchorage that is not sheltered from all winds.

Britta and Erich Neidhardt's 12-tonner *Elefant* was anchored in a bay on the east side of Neiafu in Tonga when they heard this forecast: 'Tropical cyclone Isaac, 170 miles distant, travelling south at 5 knots. Heavy rain squalls for north Tonga for tomorrow night.'

Isaac is coming straight towards them. Immediately they take countermeasures. The dinghy is brought ashore. The sprayhood is taken off. They move to a spot with perfect holding ground and anchor in 20 ft (6 m) with two heavy anchors, with 200 ft (60 m) of warp on one and 200 ft of chain on the other. At around 2000 hours the storm is 100 miles away but the full force has arrived at the anchorage. Moving about the deck of *Elefant* is only possible by crawling on all fours. At 2300 the din is immense.

'It was like the sound if you open a train window while passing through a tunnel at full speed,' Erich Neidhardt says. '*Elefant* tears at her anchors. The chain is as taut as a bar. I feel rising panic. I try desperately to keep a cool head.' They both put on several layers of clothes, collect their passports, ship's papers and money, and finally don oilskins and lifejackets. The engine is now running full ahead but the anchor chain is as taut as ever.

'Large cockroaches appear in their dozens from all corners of the boat and crawl up the starboard side. I have heard of rats leaving a sinking ship but I never knew that cockroaches have the same instinct.'

He looks around at the other few yachts anchored there. When one of them is driven ashore and sinks in 13 ft (4 m) of water, Neidhardt feels that he too will lose his boat. He recalls bitterly that this will be the second time, in the same area. Some years before his last boat was sunk by whales not far from here.

And then it happens. The engine falters, then stops. A bang like a shot indicates that the anchor chain has broken. 'A minute passes, then the second anchor begins to drag. A minute later *Elefant* drives broadside-on towards the rocky shore. Then we strike. The mast falls down in two pieces. The rudder blade flies through the air.'

As their boat strikes the steep shore the Neidhardts jump ashore, grabbing tree roots to pull themselves to safety. At one point they are caught up in the mast and shrouds as they climb up the sloping shore. Then they are safe under some trees at the top.

Next morning the storm has passed and they slide back down towards the boat. 'Below us *Elefant* lies with her port side against the rocks (the cockroaches knew to choose the starboard side). A huge rock protrudes through the side of the hull and into the water tank. The toerail is gone completely between forestay and shrouds. Bow fitting, pulpit and anchor winch have been ripped off the deck. All the stanchions are bent at a right-angle. The mast lies in two pieces between the boat and the rocks. I could cry. Below decks it is even worse. The entire cabin is under water.'

The two salvage some of the more valuable pieces of equipment, carry them up the slope and make a small tent from the remaining sails under the trees. They secure the boat as best they can and eat some tuna straight from the can and dry bread. 'We have lost all hope,' Neidhardt says of this dark hour, 'we are so tired and desperate. We feel that we cannot repair the boat here. But what can we do? We can't just put our belongings and ourselves into a container and send it home – I would never find a job back home anyway – and just leave the boat here, to be ripped to pieces by looters and thieves . . .'

However, by the next day they had recovered some of their energy and optimism. The Neidhardts started work on the boat. Some weeks later 14 parcels arrive with essential items for the boat and her equipment. Three months after the stranding *Elefant* sailed again, first to New Zealand where the repairs are finished and then on around the world and back to their home town of Flensburg in north Germany.

The French singlehanded sailor Alain Gerbault, one of the first singlehanded long-distance sailors, was incredibly lucky when his boat *Firecrest* stranded on a reef in the Wallis Islands, north of Fiji, in 1926 after the anchor warp had broken. After the boat had been pounded on the reef for an hour she capsized and Gerbault swam ashore across the lagoon beyond the reef, leaving his yacht which he thought was a total loss. But as he looked round he saw that the boat was following him! Due to the pounding on the reef the keel bolts had broken and the 4 ton ballast keel had dropped off as Gerbault was starting his swim. The boat had fallen on its side but was light enough to float over the reef towards the beach, where it arrived shortly after its owner.

Gerbault managed to repair the wooden hull. The most difficult task was to retrieve the keel from deep water beyond the reef and transport it across the lagoon to the boat. With ten newly made bolts it was eventually re-attached to the yacht, which was soon ready to set sail again. Gerbault had been helped by 50 islanders, two Chinese craftsmen and some sailors from a French warship. In due course he was to complete the solo circumnavigation in *Firecrest* for which he is remembered.

● ● ● ● ● ● ●

# Self-destruction

*A sequence of mistakes led to the unnecessary stranding of* Arcadia *in harbour in comparatively fair weather. But more unnecessary damage was done to the brand new yacht during subsequent operations to recover her.*

*Arcadia* was a standard fibreglass production cruiser on a delivery trip from the yard in France to her future home as a charter yacht in Turkey in the spring of 1985. She was 29 ft (8.85 m) long with a crew of two who were sailing her to Turkey in a series of leisurely day trips. The young skipper was meticulous in his log entries which may be an indication that he was not very experienced, at least where Greek waters were concerned. For example, he devoted a lot of space to describing the chaos typical of a Greek harbour like Mykonos as anchors were dropped on top of each other by the yachts mooring stern-on to the pier.

A few days later *Arcadia* was moored on the inner side of the pier at Kamari on Kos, not far from her final destination in Turkey. The pier runs eastwards from the shore and *Arcadia*'s berth was well sheltered from all winds from south-east through south-west to north-west. Ahead of her two more small yachts, *Jester II* and *Jester III*, were moored alongside.

The skipper of *Arcadia* woke up at midnight with an uneasy feeling. There was a swell running into the bay which found its way around the pier. The boat was quite secure in its lee and the swell was uncomfortable rather than dangerous. The other boats were more exposed to the swell, but no one on board seemed to mind. Nevertheless, *Arcadia*'s skipper woke them shortly after midnight to discuss the situation in case the wind shifted or the swell increased. He then left his berth alongside the pier and anchored a little way off, apparently under the impression that someone on one of the other boats would be on watch throughout the night.

The anchorage was only 50 yards (45 m) away from the stony beach, dead downwind. *Arcadia* was much more exposed here to swell and wind than she was previously and

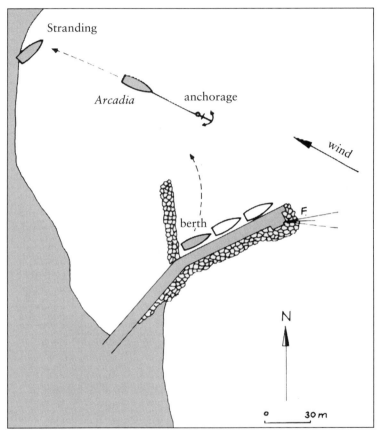

*The harbour of Kephalos on Kos showing where* Arcadia *went ashore.*

was lying to only one anchor. Her crew went to sleep relying on the crews of the other boats to keep an eye on them.

At 0445 the boat touches bottom. The anchor warp has chafed through on the bow roller. The crew start the engine and try to motor off the lee shore but without success. At 0500 a fishing boat tries to tow them off but in the course of the manoeuvre she too touches bottom, damages her rudder and propeller, and has to be towed off by another fishing boat. The wind is now south-west force 5.

At 0700 a mechanical digger is employed to drag *Arcadia* up on to the beach. Around midday it pulls her even further ashore in case the wind should increase. While the well-rested crews of the other two boats begin another day's sailing, *Arcadia* is not only high and dry on the beach but has been damaged considerably by being pulled across the stones. The rudder is split in half, the keel has been partly detached from the hull, and the hull itself has been stove-in and damaged over a wide area of the port side where she was pulled along. An additional problem is the fact that the necessary repairs cannot be done on this small, rather remote island.

Temporary repairs were effected locally and she was re-launched to be sailed to her destination in Turkey weeks later. At least it can be said that the incident gave a boost to the island's economy, not to mention the yard in Turkey which carried out the permanent repairs.

It could all so easily have been avoided. The skipper need never have anchored off the lee shore. When he did so he should have maintained an anchor watch with the engine ready to start. The anchor rope should have been protected against chafe or doubled up. It would have been advisable to drop a second anchor anyway. After the stranding it would have been better to leave the boat in the water, secured by another anchor (if necessary borrowed from a fishing boat), rather than drag her ashore and cause much worse damage.

● ● ● ● ● ● ●

# Out of the blue

*The catamaran* Gust *had been dried out deliberately on a picturesque beach in the Channel Islands. Her troubles began when the tide rose again. Her fate dramatically illustrates the risks of drying out on an exposed beach, even if the sea appears to be calm.*

A solidly built fibreglass cruising catamaran of a well-proven design, *Gust* was a 30 ft (9 m) Catalac. She had been built in 1979 and had been sailed by her owner, Ulf Wille, several times before on cruises in the English Channel. This typical cruising catamaran has an abundance of space on and below deck, but it can also take the ground easily with a draft of only 2 ft 7 in (80 cm). When dried out she stands upright like a sledge on her two keels.

In the summer of 1984 Wille was on a return visit to the Channel Islands with a friend. It was a fine sailing day with a gentle breeze. Towards midday they anchored in the bay of La Grande Grève on Sark. They chose a spot close to the steep shore on a strip of hard sand that would be exposed at low water. The catamaran was moored with her bows towards the shore and two anchors laid out astern in the form of a large 'V'.

Two hours later it was high water. With spring tides and a tidal range of 20 ft (6 m), *Gust* now had about 7 ft (2 m) of water under her keels. As the tide fell the crew went ashore to have dinner. 'Neither the wind nor the sea had changed during the past five hours,' says Wille. 'Within 30 minutes of our leaving, *Gust* would dry out as planned.

'When we returned around midnight she was sitting on the firm sand. We cleared the propellers and shafts. Then we noticed a significant increase in the swell that was coming into the bay even though the wind direction and strength had not changed. We were quite surprised by this development as we had not noticed anything that would account for this sudden increase in swell.'

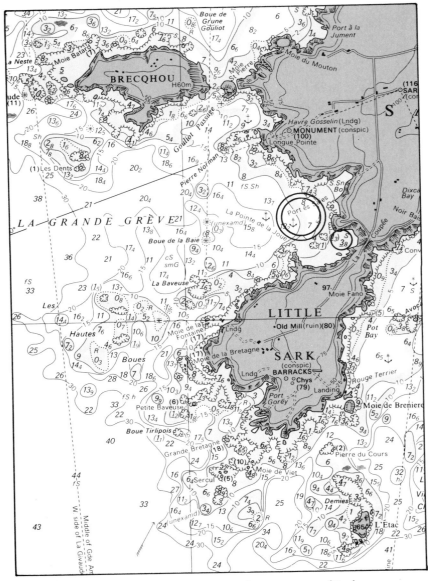

*Chart of La Grande Grève on the west coast of Sark.*
*Circles show the recognized anchorage (double circle) and*
*the place where* Gust *dried out (single circle).*

In anticipation of problems, they re-laid one of the anchors as far to seaward as possible. But this was about all they could do, except watch the further course of events. 'With the incoming tide the height of the waves quickly increased to 6 to 10 ft [2 to 3 m]. It became clear that *Gust* would be in serious trouble as she refloated. When the water reached the boat the breaking seas quickly filled the engine compartments aft and cabins.

'On board I noticed that she would float for an instant on the crests of the breakers, but the anchors must have dragged and she was being pushed further and further up the shore. Shortly afterwards breakers started to sweep the entire deck so that remaining on board became seriously dangerous. I took the most important papers and left *Gust*. Then some people arrived on the scene to help, and together we tried to put out another anchor to seaward with a small inflatable, but this proved to be impossible. We could then only watch from the shore as she was smashed on the rocks. Around 0200 the starboard hull broke in the middle. Shortly afterwards the port hull followed suit.'

All that was left eventually of the catamaran was a scattered heap of wood splinters and shredded fibreglass. The violence of the breakers may be deduced from the fact that one of the diesel engines was found 5 yards (4.5 m) away from the other remains of the boat.

The insurance company took the view that Wille had been negligent by ignoring the fact that in such an area the seas could build up even without an increase in wind. Indeed, if he had known this, it certainly would have been irresponsible to have dried out where he did.

On the other hand, he could point to the fact that he had had experience of these waters on previous cruises. He had anchored in the same bay several times in other years and had dried out without any problems in comparable weather conditions. The bay is clearly marked as an anchorage on the chart and in the pilot. It is sheltered from north-west through north-east to south-east by the surrounding rocks. There was no obvious reason for Wille to regard the anchorage as unsafe that night.

However, *Gust* was anchored close to the shore, not in the spot marked as an anchorage. There is a depth there of 20 ft (6 m) at low water and it is at least 200 yards (180 m) away from the shore. If she had been afloat at low water *Gust* would probably have been unharmed.

In recognition of the arguments on both sides, a court eventually awarded Wille half the amount of his insurance claim.

• • • • • • • •

# A providential outcome

*It can be surprisingly hard to translate theoretical knowledge into the right action in a real emergency. Judith Lowe described an experience of this on a passage to France in the family yacht* Providence *and the rather satisfactory outcome of their potentially disastrous grounding.*

It is useful to learn, from a real emergency, how quickly the theoretical knowledge of what one should do is actually transferred into practical action in the dark hours of night on a heaving sea. The English yachtswoman Judith Lowe once described this feeling quite interestingly. This is her story.

The Lowes were sailing with their three children from Walton-on-the-Naze, north of the Thames estuary, to Calais. Their yacht *Providence* was a 30 ft (9 m) bilge-keeler.

Around midnight her husband woke her for her watch. *Providence* was about a mile south-west of the Long Sand Head buoy, marking one of the many long narrow shoals off the Thames estuary, on a cold wet summer's night.

They had chosen this slightly risky course, cutting across the end of the bank, to save distance and sailing time. It was about an hour before low water and they would have less than a metre of water under the keel at low water.

When Lowe had donned pullover and oilskins she started to brew up a cup of tea as was her usual routine. But suddenly her husband knocked nervously on the hatch and said, 'There's no time for tea now. We have an emergency!' After Judith jumped into the cockpit he explained, 'We are passing over the end of Long Sand. I think we may not have enough water. The sounder only shows one metre.'

Lowe was alarmed. The wind was light and *Providence* was motoring but there was still a nasty left-over swell from an earlier force 6. The yacht was heading straight into the seas, ducking her bows into the oncoming swells.

'Read out the depths on the sounder,' he said and she began, 'Okay ... still one metre ... point seven ... point eight ... zero,' she held her breath, '... point six ... point six ... still point six ... zero again ...' and they hit bottom with a shudder. They were aground and a wave broke against the hull. The boat rose and came down hard on the bottom again.

'Go below and wake up the children and help them put on their lifejackets,' he said in a voice betraying tenseness. 'Give me the VHF microphone and my lifejacket. And put on yours, too.'

As she was waking the children he had the microphone in one hand but on a sudden impulse was trying to sound the depth with the lead line with the other at the same time.

'Wake up, children, and put on your lifejackets.' Still half-asleep, they asked, 'What's happening, Mum?'

After a second's hesitation she answered, 'Nothing ... yet. But we are touching bottom and we may have to get in the liferaft.' Still very sleepy, the children sat up in their bunks. But then all of a sudden they said simply, 'Good night, Mummy,' and went back to sleep.

Lowe was dazed. On her way back to the cockpit she wondered whether it was time to send out a MAYDAY. Or should one say PAN PAN or SECURITÉ instead? What were the exact meanings of these words and what was the difference between them?

Before she could think any more, the boat bumped hard on the bottom twice more. A wave broke clean over the yacht and water came cascading into the cockpit. Her husband had stopped depth-sounding because he was having to hold on to the boat with one hand. With his free hand he lifted the microphone to his mouth and called, 'SECURITÉ. SECURITÉ. SECURITÉ. Thames coastguard. This is *Providence, Providence, Providence*. Position about one mile south-west of Long Sand Head buoy. We are aground and waves are breaking over us. Over.'

They waited for a reply but nothing happened. Both had the same thought: 'They are asleep and not listening.' Another sea filled the cockpit. She said, 'Why don't they answer?'

Silence again. Then it dawned on him, 'Damn. I forgot to press the transmit button. Nothing went out.' For a moment they looked at one another. He grinned apologetically. But just as he was about to try again the boat suddenly moved forwards. The echo sounder flickered ... one metre ... then two. The boat motored forwards. They were past the shoal. 'We're over!' he cried with relief and then added, 'Okay, darling, put the flares away. Let's have tea now. And then it's your watch. And always remember: *Never panic*.'

Were they right to try and call the coastguard? In most ways they were. In an emergency it is always preferable to call the coastguard too early rather than too late. And it is right to inform the coastguard if the situation is unclear and could develop into an emergency later on. Thus far, *Providence*'s skipper did the right thing.

But, of course, he should not have used the word SECURITÉ. This precedes broadcasts of navigational information. *Providence* should have transmitted a PAN PAN call as she was in a dangerous but not distress situation. If things had turned out less satisfactorily for them, the coast radio station would have coordinated whatever assistance was required without launching a full-scale rescue operation, as would be done with a MAYDAY call. A MAYDAY obliges all vessels in the vicinity to go to the rescue in the interests of saving life. An unjustified MAYDAY call can cause considerable expense.

# 3
# SINKING

## Achilles' heel

*A centreboard can clearly be an asset to a yacht that operates in shoal waters but it can also be a weakness, even in a heavily built steel yacht. This proved to be the case with* Freizeit *which sank off the Frisian Islands after an apparently minor brush with a mudbank.*

Willi Koopman's dream yacht was built very heavily in steel. The flat bottom of the 41 ft (12.5 m) centreboarder was 15 mm (0.59 in) thick, the bilges 8 mm (0.32 in), the topsides 6 mm (0.24 in). There was a midships centreboard casing welded to the bottom plates which housed a 4 ton drop keel suspended from a bolt in the leading edge, operated hydraulically. Further strengthening in this area was achieved by the diesel tanks which were fitted across the full width of the boat and were like a double bottom.

Koopman's home waters are the islands of the German North Sea coast and the tidal waters behind them. All seemed well on a fine summer's weekend in August 1982 with a north-easterly breeze and a few clouds in the sky. A particular hazard of these waters are the short choppy seas, coupled with a heavy ground swell and breakers where the waves come in from deep water and run into the shallows. *Freizeit* was coping with these seas, as she beat up the Minsener Rinne, near the island of Wangerooge, with her centreboard lowered to its maximum draft of 8 ft 10 in (2.7 m). As she tacked she met a particularly nasty wave and she ended up bumping hard on the bottom in the swell a few times. Koopman checked the bilges afterwards and found them dry.

It later emerged that the bumps occurred as the boat was drifting astern, having missed stays, and again while she was moving forwards again slowly gathering way. But having checked the bilges and being full of confidence in his strongly built boat, Koopman sailed on. But when his crew went below a little later the water had already risen above the floor boards. Koopman started pumping and transmitted a PAN PAN call. *Freizeit* was now north of the channel. The water could not be kept at bay with pumps and buckets.

Soon the lifeboat *Wilhelm Kaysen* arrived on the scene. She handed over a large electric pump and took *Freizeit* in tow. The crews of both boats thought that the worst was over as the electric pump slowly lowered the water level in the boat. But then the electric cable parted and the water started rising rapidly. Koopman and his crew had to abandon the boat which soon sank in 45 ft (14 m) of water with only the top of the mast showing above the surface. The lifeboat broadcast a warning to shipping and requested a wreck-buoy.

The yacht was now on the bottom of the North Sea, still intact. She was worth salvaging as only her engine and electrics would be damaged. The insurance company hired a salvage company for the job and a week later work began.

A floating crane was anchored over the wreck while divers checked how she was lying. She was leaning to one side, as could be seen from the mast. The bows were buried in the sand. The stern was free. They decided to use steel cables instead of nylon strops to lift her.

Despite the calm weather there was a slight swell running. In these conditions the boat could not be raised completely. With her stern above water but the bows still below, she was towed back towards port at an angle of 45°. But as the floating crane entered shallower water near Mellum the bows touched bottom. The bowsprit was bent and the mizenmast broke.

*Water gushes out of the damaged centreboard case as* Freizeit *is craned out. Seconds later, a lifting strop broke and the yacht crashed on to the quayside, damaged beyond repair.*

After hoisting her up a bit the weight of the boat was reduced with the help of a high capacity pump, but despite these efforts *Freizeit* was still too heavy to be lifted on deck. The tow continued with the yacht hanging from the crane alongside, while a larger crane was ordered for the final destination of Hooksiel.

As the larger crane raised the yacht, now with slings of nylon webbing, everyone heaved a sigh of relief. Slowly the bilges with the still lowered centreboard rose above the surface. A jet of water rushed out of the centreboard casing and then the forward sling broke at the eye.

The bows crashed on to the quayside, while the stern slid back into the water. Under the impact the mainmast broke into several pieces, the rail was bent and the hull damaged externally. In view of the damage already sustained, *Freizeit* was ultimately a write-off.

The financial loss was covered by the yacht's and the salvage company's insurers. It is interesting to note why she sank in the first place. This is the surveyor's report:

> According to the owner, the boat touched bottom while tacking and she was actually moving astern. The keel was pushed forwards against the front of the casing. A deep notch in the lead keel still shows this. At the same time, as the hydraulic ram was now extended too far, the rod buckled and came out of the cylinder.
>
> After the first grounding, skipper Koopman started the engine but grounded again, though with how much force he cannot recall. On this second grounding the boat moved forwards over the keel, forcing it upwards like a hinge back into the casing. Koopman recalls a loud bang at this moment which must have been the centreboard casing parting.

The end of the hydraulic cylinder, having nothing to support it after the connecting rod had come out, was hanging down into the centreboard casing. When the keel was pushed up by running aground for the second time, the cylinder was in its way. So the keel forced it forwards and upwards, causing the

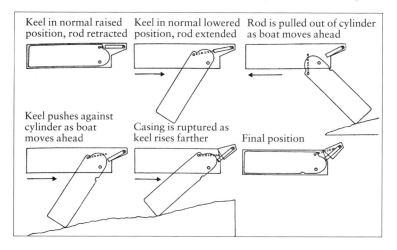

Keel in normal raised position, rod retracted

Keel in normal lowered position, rod extended

Rod is pulled out of cylinder as boat moves ahead

Keel pushes against cylinder as boat moves ahead

Casing is ruptured as keel rises farther

Final position

front of the casing to burst open. The surveyor concluded that the resulting leak had an area of about 30 sq in (200 sq cm).

It is perhaps worth pointing out that a hole of even a tenth of that size, if it was 20 in (50 cm) below the waterline, would have admitted water faster than it could have been pumped out by hand. If the hole envisaged by the surveyor had been at that depth *Freizeit* would have sunk within four minutes, which would have been too quickly for the lifeboat to reach her. However, assuming the leak was only about 8 in (20 cm) below the surface, the inflow would have been about 55 gallons (250 litres) per minute. If the crew managed to pump out 22 gallons (100 litres) per minute the yacht would have taken about 80 minutes to sink, which gave the lifeboat time to arrive.

• • • • • • •

# Lost at sea

*The sinking of* Tina *off north-east Scotland, after she had been discovered motoring round in circles with no sign of her singlehanded skipper, is an illustration of the limitations of a large vessel in rendering assistance to a yacht.*

Fritz Heimann had an ambitious plan. He wanted to sail singlehanded from Germany to the Faeroes and back. His daughter and son-in-law would run his business in his absence, so there was plenty of time available.

His yacht *Tina* was a standard production centreboarder built in England, with a length of 32 ft 8 in (9.95 m) and a beam of 11 ft 10 in (3.6 m). The boat displaced five tons, had 500 sq ft (46 m²) of working sail area and a Bukh 36 hp diesel engine.

His daughter was there to see him off on 22 August 1984. 'Bye-bye,' she called to him, 'Be careful.' 'Don't worry,' he replied, 'I will be very careful – I'm taking no chances. See you again soon!'

But at this moment, neither of them knew that they had seen each other for the last time.

Six days later *Tina* passed the oil platform DF97, on latitude 58°N, 140 miles off the coast of Scotland. The crew of the platform looked down at the small boat and waved back to the lone sailor at the helm. This was the last anyone saw of him.

Not quite two days later the Danish trawler *Auskerry* from Esbjerg sighted the boat. Skipper Jens Mose Jensen was at the wheel and at first he took no more than a casual glance at the yacht. But then he had a second look. The sea was rough that day with a force 7 wind. The yacht seemed to be lying a-hull. But then he realized that she was making way and steering an erratic course. Through the binoculars he could see that she was motoring in circles and there was nobody on deck.

Out of habit he glanced at the clock in the wheelhouse as he pushed the throttle forward and changed course slightly. It was 0800 on a fine but windy summer's day. As *Auskerry* neared the circling yacht Jensen could see that the navigation lights were on. The helm was hard over to one side and there was a line trailing in the yacht's wake.

Alerted by the change of course and increased speed, two crew members had by now appeared at Jensen's side. In a few words and with some explanatory waves of his hand, he explained the situation and his intention to try and go alongside the yacht in an attempt to find out what had happened.

But the attempt failed. It was of course quite difficult to approach a yacht in the rough conditions, especially one that was motoring in circles. It would have been impossible to do so without causing damage, particularly to the yacht. Jensen decided to alert the British coastguard.

At 0930 he transmitted: 'Sighted apparently unmanned yacht. Name: *Tina*. In position 58°25'N and 000°48'E. The yacht is motoring and turning in circles. The navigation lights are on. A line is trailing astern. Wind west-south-west 42 knots. Seas 16 feet. Weather fair.'

This was the end of the matter for *Auskerry* who continued her trip. The coast radio station immediately informed the

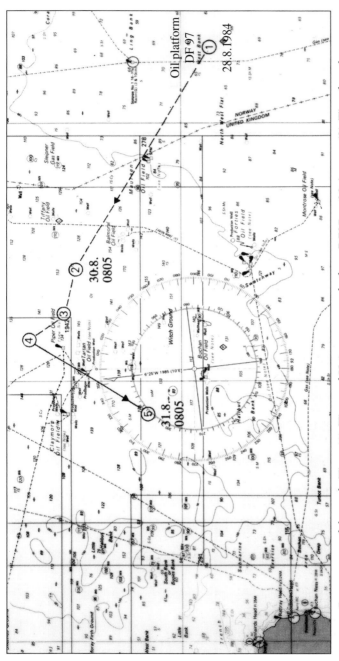

*Last voyage of the yacht* Tina. (*1*) Tina *and Heimann pass platform DF97 on 28 August.* (*2*) Tina *found motoring in circles by trawler Auskerry at 0805 on 30 August.* (*3*) Tina *located by support vessel Northern Clipper.* (*4*) *Northern Clipper starts towing yacht towards Peterhead.* (*5*) Tina *sinks at 0805 on 31 August.*

93

coastguard who took over responsibility for *Tina*. The control centre at Peterhead, on the east coast of Scotland, requested the Norwegian oil rig support vessel *Northern Clipper*, which was standing by the Piper Alpha platform, to investigate. The following are extracts from *Northern Clipper*'s log:

*Thursday 30 August, 0755* Alongside Piper Alpha. Commence unloading cargo.

*0830* Finish unloading. Back to stand-by position.

*1050* The British coastguard asks us to go 17 miles to the east where an abandoned yacht has been sighted.

*1052* Leave stand-by position. Full speed ahead. Weather SW 7. Seas 12 to 15 feet.

*1210* Have reached the yacht. She is motoring in circles.

*1220* It has been possible to ship over a crew member to the yacht. Due to the weather it is very difficult to attach a tow line. After two unsuccessful attempts we decide to put a second crew member on the yacht, with a portable VHF as the yacht has no VHF set.

*1400* The second crew is on the yacht. We try for a third time to pass a tow but the line breaks. Part of the line fouls our starboard propeller. So we decide that the yacht shall proceed under her own power. For this purpose diesel has to be shipped over to her. This takes until 1500 hours.

*1510* Set a course for Piper Alpha. 278°. Distance now 26 miles. We are following the yacht, which motors at 3 knots. The crew on the yacht inform us that she is making water through her damaged bow, where the deck has parted from the hull. Apparently the forestay has caused this damage. A sharp lookout for survivors is maintained throughout.

*2000* The search for survivors is abandoned.

*2250* Have reached Piper Alpha. We leave the yacht adrift

outside the 200 yard zone with two crew on board while going alongside.

*2350* Leaving Piper Alpha to tow the yacht to Peterhead.

*2400* We take the yacht alongside and secure a tow. The line is belayed to the foot of the mast and led forward, with a second safety line, which passes through the forehatch.

*Friday 31 August, 0050* We take the two crew back on board and start the tow towards Peterhead. The weather has moderated. West force 5. Seas now 8 to 10 feet.

*0350* As the tow proceeds the yacht is settling deeper and deeper into the water.

*0500* At daybreak we decide to put three men on the yacht to pump her out, but this proves impossible. The mast has been ripped from its step and water has been flowing in for hours through a leak at this point.

*0600* We have managed to bring the yacht alongside once more and try to lift her with our crane. But due to the seas it is impossible to keep her alongside for long enough. We have to abandon the attempt at lifting her.

*0730* We secure another tow rope to the yacht in such a way as to lift her bows and we start towing again, but after 15 minutes the yacht has settled down so far that her decks are below water.

*0805* Sinking of the German sailing yacht *Tina* in position 58°05'N and 000°14'W. *Northern Clipper* continues to Peterhead.

*1500* Arrival in Peterhead. Divers check our starboard propeller and remove line from it. Some personal belongings taken from the yacht before she sank are handed over to the police.

Meanwhile the rescue co-ordination centre had broadcast a distress message requesting shipping in the area to search for the crew of the yacht, whose number was at that point still unknown. Aircraft were also involved in the search. In total, seven ships, three helicopters and two aircraft search the area around the first sighting of the yacht to no avail. The search is called off on 31 August at 0900.

One can only speculate about what happened to Heimann. It seems probable that he fell overboard while working on deck, probably on the night of 29/30 August (this seems likely in view of the navigation lights being on).

The fact that the yacht was not sailing but running under engine can be explained by the damage to her bows. Perhaps Heimann was trying to fix the problem. It seems the attachment of the forestay and the bonding of the deck to the hull at this critical point were not strong enough to cope with sailing to windward in strong winds.

This episode also clearly shows that large ships have difficulty towing small yachts. The latter seldom have deck fittings strong enough to take the exceptional strain of being towed by a ship. The mast step on *Tina* had obviously been designed to cope with strong vertical loads but not to withstand even stronger horizontal forces.

It might have been possible to let the yacht make her own way to Peterhead with some crew of *Northern Clipper* on board, perhaps even repairing the leak in the bows, at least temporarily, enough to reduce or stop water entering. But merchant seamen are seldom yachtsmen and they are understandably reluctant to exchange their working environment on a ship for a fragile, swaying yacht.

• • • • • • •

# Stress and distress

*Tranquillizers have yet to become a part of the distress equipment of the average yacht. The bizarre story of Werner and Gundi struggling with suppositories on their sinking boat may help to explain why.*

Bärbel Bahlcke is an experienced blue water yachtswoman. With her husband she has completed many long passages, including a circumnavigation on their 29 ft 6 in (9 m) cruising yacht. It was therefore surprising to hear her say, 'Whenever the weather gets too nasty or a particularly unpleasant situation arises, I take my Valium and retire to my bunk.'

'Did I understand you correctly? When things get difficult you take a tranquillizer and lie down?'

'Yes,' she replied, 'Rather than endure a prolonged crisis.'

'And your husband?' 'He can cope alone. Maybe better!'

I looked at him and he nodded. It may be difficult, but it is possible to understand her attitude. After all she is able to enjoy blue water sailing by blotting out the unpleasant bits with the aid of Valium and sleep. At the same time her husband may find it easier to get on with sailing the boat, uninhibited by his wife.

But it is a different matter if both husband and wife, in this case the entire crew of the boat, try to calm themselves down with tranquillizers in a distress situation. Using drugs to soothe the nerves or try and overcome fear means reducing circulation to a minimum, thereby sacrificing the capacity for quick and sharp mental reaction as well as physical strength.

Gundi and Werner had both been sailing for many years, racing in their home waters as well as cruising in the Mediterranean. Outward bound in the winter of 1982/83 on another cruise starting from southern Spain, they headed south for the African coast near Melilla. The forecast promised a quiet night, the Spanish island of Alboran with its strong light would be a good visual mark after dark.

But the forecast proved to be wrong. The westerly force 3 of the morning soon increased to force 5 or 6 in the afternoon, reaching force 7 at night. It also backed south-west so that they could not hold their course. Soon the boat was sailing under storm jib only and when they decided to run before the wind on the other tack they were unable to go about.

Werner tried to start the engine to help the small boat through the wind, but the batteries were too low. They decided to gybe round on to the new course.

Although the gybe was successful both backstays parted immediately afterwards. The mast bent like a reed and by the time Werner had started to rig the topping lift as a temporary backstay the mast had worked itself loose from its step and gone over the side. Werner now tried to secure the mast alongside by lashing it to the stanchions. He was only partly successful, wrenching his wrist in the process. It was a difficult job for one person. With Gundi to help him it would have been much easier to secure the long aluminium spar, with spreaders and boom, alongside. And perhaps by lashing the spar satisfactorily the ensuing leak in the hull could have been avoided, possibly changing the whole course of events.

However, Gundi was not available at this critical juncture. After the mast came down she was busy searching the cabin for something to help them get over the dreadful experience: their tranquillizers.

Obviously, the insertion of a suppository when wearing a lifejacket over a one-piece suit on a boat tossing in the waves is not easy and takes time. And all the time she was thus engaged, the mast was bashing against the hull, slowly opening a leak in the side. Spray was also entering the cabin through the open companionway as the boat was stern-on to the wind, but as yet not much water had come on board.

When Gundi had finished, her husband went through the same procedure. This meant that he had to leave the temporarily lashed mast and retreat to the cabin. While he in turn was struggling out of his wet gear the mast continued to hammer against the hull at a point behind a hanging locker which would be virtually impossible to reach when the need arose to stuff the leak.

By now the water was rising alarmingly fast inside the boat. Minutes later Werner had trouble finding the strength to dismantle the wardrobe in an attempt to reach the leak. He felt weak and exhausted, believing it to be due to his injured wrist, but one wonders whether this was really the reason.

Gundi was now bailing with a bucket. Werner gave up trying to plug the leak and pumped as best he could. But with the boat lying stern to the wind, most of the water that Gundi threw out through the open companionway instantly found its way back in again. The water continued to rise and the two soon ended their attempts, mentally and physically exhausted. With their last remaining energy they launched the liferaft and tied it to the boat. As dawn broke they fired several flares and two ships close by offered the prospect of rescue and safety.

Gundi was first to board the raft, whereupon it was blown away to the full extent of the long painter. Nervousness caused mistakes. Werner made it into the raft, but they found themselves unable to cast off. With their teeth, they managed to open the bag containing vital items that included a knife. Eventually they succeeded in cutting the painter and freeing themselves from the boat. To their despair their troubles were not over. The sea anchor was fitted in exactly the wrong place, holding the opening of the raft into the wind so the inside was flooded by spray. With the zip closed it was impossible to bail the raft out; with it open more water came in. They tried to move the sea anchor to the other side of the raft but their exhausted state made it impossible.

Their physical weakness caused more problems when they finally came alongside one of the ships. The ship's crew expected them to be able to climb a rope boarding ladder hanging down the side but neither of them was able to do this.

Somehow they were finally heaved up on to the deck of the ship to safety. Their boat had sunk in the meantime. A few hours later they were put ashore at a Spanish port and taken to hospital where they were treated for exhaustion. A doctor draws the following conclusion from this episode:

Tranquillizers depress the activity of the central nervous system. They slow down reactions and events are perceived by the person concerned as if from a distance. The intensity of these symptoms varies with the dosage and the degree to which the body might already be accustomed to the drug. In this case there may have been an addiction as it would otherwise be unlikely that the first thing people do in an emergency is take tranquillizers.

In general, medicines should be taken to treat illness. Modern tranquillizers are effective at combating excessive fear or psychological stress. But unfortunately the question is too seldom raised of whether the symptoms really amount to an illness or if the patient would in the end be as well off without the drug. When taken while sailing it must be clear that these drugs impair judgement and dramatically slow one's reactions. The belief that one is able to cope better with a distress situation under their influence is completely and dangerously mistaken.

• • • • • • •

## Stay with the boat

*A yacht, even one that is half-sunk, stands a much better chance of being found than a small dinghy. This is demonstrated by the following story in which the yacht is instrumental in her owner's rescue even though he is several miles away.*

On his elderly 21 ft (6.5 m) pocket cruiser Gerhard Schulze left Arnis on the river Schlei in the Baltic bound for the island of Fehmarn on a short singlehanded passage in April 1985. 'Until 0200 hours, everything went smoothly,' he recalls, 'Then a crash at the bow shook the boat, but I didn't worry about it at first.'

After a while he noticed that the boat was making water. 'I don't know what caused the leak, maybe driftwood. I could not locate it as it was behind the lockers. By now the water was pouring into the boat and I could not keep up with it by bailing. I had to abandon ship and boarded my rubber dinghy which had been inflated in less than five minutes by the compressor. I threw my distress kit on board, along with some warm clothes and oilskins, and left the boat.'

The fact that he was found and picked up seven hours later by an SAR helicopter is due to the boat he had abandoned. She did not sink, as he had presumed, but was picked up four hours later by a Danish cargo ship. The small cruiser was keel-up but still afloat. Her discovery caused the alarm to be raised which finally led to the owner's rescue. With a bit more luck the upturned boat might even have been towed into harbour by the lifeboat. She finally sank only after a prolonged tow.

The position where Schulze was picked up in his dinghy was several miles away from where the boat was found so the rescuers did not see his distress signals until the search area had been considerably enlarged.

So the old rule holds true. No matter how hopeless the situation may seem, *stay with the boat until she sinks*. Even if it means being in the dinghy or liferaft attached to the boat by a long rope ready to be cut or cast off.

# 4
# ABANDONED YACHTS

---

## *Think before you leap*

*The annals of yachting contain many accounts of boats being kept afloat against all the odds. The epic story of the* Joan *in 1927 is a good example. Today's yachtsmen seem altogether less reluctant to abandon their vessels, tragically sometimes losing their lives in cases where the yacht is later found afloat.*

We are all grateful for the highly efficient rescue services which exist especially in north European waters. Without a doubt more and more yachtsmen are being rescued by them, the increasing numbers reflecting the increasing popularity of the sport. Many lives and many yachts have been saved. The dangerous work performed by the members of the rescue services of all countries must command our highest undiluted respect and appreciation.

On the other hand, I would like to make the perhaps controversial point that the availability of this highly efficient and reliable service has sometimes led people to transmit premature MAYDAY calls and rely on rescue by the professionals, without having first tried to resolve the situation by their own efforts. In other parts of the world, however, such a service is more often than not either totally unavailable or less sophisticated and reliable. Under these circumstances it is necessary to fight for survival and try to save the yacht and nurse her into port, which only seldom will be her original destination. And if after losing the fight you have to resort to the liferaft you may have to survive in the small unstable craft for days or even weeks before being picked up.

An example of endurance in fighting for survival is the last voyage of the *Joan*, a wooden yawl of only 22 ft (6.8 m) length. Skipper Sinclair and his crew Meredith Jackson finally abandoned ship on 7 September 1927 about 350 miles north-east of the Belle Isle Strait between Newfoundland and Labrador.

The yacht had a self-draining cockpit but no forehatch or skylight. Water could only enter the cabin via the companionway, apart of course from the seams of the wooden hull, the keel bolt holes and all the other weak points of ageing wooden boats of traditional construction exposed to severe seas. However, *Joan* was by the standards of 1927 a solidly built seaworthy cruiser when she set off on her voyage from London to Reykjavik. On 12 August she left Iceland bound for St John's, Newfoundland. The next three weeks were extremely hard sailing, bearing in mind that this was a boat the size of an Etap 22 or Sunbeam 23 with less space below decks, exposed to the violence and massive seas of the North Atlantic. Moreover, the boat was heavily loaded with equipment and stores.

'After days of exhausting sailing, we always found it a relief when we had to heave-to for as many days and could at least catch up with our sleep,' Jackson wrote. 'On 1 September we were lying to the sea anchor and hoping for better weather soon. But we waited in vain. The gale blew as hard as only a gale in these waters can and the sea was so rough that it seemed it could scarcely be worse. But towards evening the gale increased and the seas got even wilder. I have since heard that we were caught on the edge of a hurricane but even on that September evening in those indescribable hurricane force conditions I never thought that anything would happen to us. As soon as I had finished my watch I retired to my bunk and soon fell asleep.

'I cannot clearly remember what awoke me around ten at night. There was an incredible din all around me and I found myself out of the bunk, somewhere in the cabin. Everything was inky black. "This is the end," I thought. I became almost impatient as I was still able to think and nothing had happened.

'Then my full consciousness returned and when I eventually tried to open the companionway hatch my hands found a gaping hole in the deck.

'Sinclair was already in the cockpit, saying that the mainmast had gone. I saw the mast drifting dangerously close to the hull and we quickly cut the rigging to prevent further damage. We then bailed the water from the cabin back into the Atlantic. By around one at night the decks were clear and the boat bailed out. But *Joan* was leaking so badly that one of us had to keep up the bailing, while the other nailed blankets and sails over the hull and deck.'

The *Joan* had capsized. In righting herself she had not only lost her mainmast but received gaping wounds in hull and deck. Although she was heavily built her iron keel bolts had bent and she was now leaking seriously in a place well below the waterline that was impossible to reach or repair at sea.

Just as temporary repairs were being finished on 4 September, a new hurricane assaulted the small craft and in the ensuing seas *Joan* leaked even more than before. Nothing could be done to steady her in the waves, as neither a scrap of sail nor a sea anchor could be employed. Still, the two men survived under appalling conditions on the tiny vessel by bailing continuously. There was no alternative; the nearest coast was nearly 350 miles away to windward.

'But we had some material for a jury rig and enough food,' Jackson continues. 'The rationed water would last us for another 80 days. And when the blow finally ceased we set our smallest jib between the bow and the top of the mizenmast and crept slowly but surely onwards on a south-westerly course.

'However, we had not succeeded in making the hull watertight and so we could not sail for 24 hours a day. At the end of each watch the sail was lowered and the man on watch had to bail out for over an hour. Only then was the other roused from his berth. He in turn had to follow the same procedure at the end of his watch.

'This is how we managed until the evening of 7 September. We were, by chance, both in the cockpit when we sighted a steamer south of us. We both knew what to do. *Joan* had suffered too much damage, had nearly no value, and we would take at least another two weeks to sail this floating wreck to the land. So we fired our flares and let ourselves be taken aboard the only ship that had crossed our wake in this waste of water. *Joan* would have sunk soon after, leaking as she was and with her companionway open.'

The two men had sailed their diminutive craft through nearly four weeks of gales and heavy weather, mountainous seas, a capsize and dismasting, resulting in leaks which necessitated almost continuous bailing. It is a remarkable story of survival against the odds. And if they had not encountered the steamer one can well believe that they would have succeeded in reaching the Canadian coast.

What a complete contrast to the charter yacht that sailed from Bornholm for Klintholm in the late summer of 1985 which was abandoned while afloat and still sailing. Four men were sailing the Swedish-built long-keeled Vindö 45 cruiser back from Gotland to Denmark. This 33 ft (10 m) yacht was a sturdy example of a Scandinavian cruiser with a powerful engine. On their way back they had stopped over in Rønne, Bornholm, and left there at noon one day in early September with the forecast of south-westerly to westerly winds of force 6 to 7 with squally showers. They knew that their destination was 80 miles dead to windward and that they would have to beat into strong winds for around 50 hours, with a favourable windshift a bit less, with an increase of wind a bit more.

The wind soon shifted, as forecast, to west then north-west. During the night the squalls reached force 8. The boat was making limited headway under triple-reefed main and small working jib.

When the wind increased the following morning and the jib blew out with a bang the crew contacted a Danish coast station, but they quite rightly declined the offer of a rescue helicopter. What was the problem? The boat was completely undamaged. Just a jib was torn. The coast to leeward was at least 20, more probably 50, miles away, so there was no danger from that. And with the wind veering to north-west, the boat would have ample sea room to turn and run off downwind or heave-to if it should become necessary. Of course, they would have had to abandon their plan to reach Klintholm for the time being.

But the skipper believed that the risk of injury was too high for those on board. When a Polish cargo ship came within sight he called her up and had himself and his crew taken off the boat. They were landed at Gdynia. The abandoned and undamaged yacht meanwhile sailed on under mainsail and engine and ran ashore on a sandy beach in Poland 77 miles away about 38 hours later.

It would perhaps be unfair to apply the same standards to the crew of a charter yacht as to the crew of the *Joan*, but the same rule applies, *Don't leave the boat unnecessarily*. To abandon a seaworthy yacht with no more damage than a torn jib is bad seamanship by any standards.

And not all yachtsmen who look for safety in the shape of a passing ship find it. Two yachtsmen died when their yacht *Evolution II* went alongside the German freighter *Cap San Antonio* in the English Channel in May 1977. Only three of the crew of five managed to climb to safety. In November of the same year a crew member of the French yacht *Algae* was crushed between the yacht and the ship's side as he attempted to climb a boarding ladder. A woman was trapped between a ship and her yacht *Samos* in December 1980. Her life was only saved by the ship's captain at the cost of the yacht, which had been undamaged when she came alongside.

And even getting from a liferaft on to the deck of a ship is fraught with danger. In the notorious Fastnet Race of 1979 the crew of *Ariadne* had abandoned the yacht and taken to the liferaft after the boat had been rolled through 360°, losing one man and the mast. A couple of hours later the German freighter *Nanna* made three attempts to save the five survivors. Tragically only two made it on to the ship. The other three perished when the liferaft was sucked into the ship's propeller.

The risk to life when abandoning a yacht is even present when sailing near the coast or, indeed, when at anchor. It takes experience to make the right decision in times of stress and

Ariadne, *dismasted but still afloat after the 1979 Fastnet Race storm. Four members of her six-man crew were lost, three of them perished after they had taken to the liferaft.*

imminent danger. An initial assessment is not always the best.

On 16 May 1963 the converted 12 metre *Sylvia* was motoring along the coast of Corsica with foresails stowed below decks and mainsail furled on the boom under its cover. The wind was very fresh and the crew did not plan to do any sailing. When the engine stopped suddenly they found themselves close in to a lee shore without time to make sail. They let go both anchors. The warp of the smaller anchor, which was used first, snapped when it came tight. The main anchor appeared to offer little chance of salvation as it was broken.

As the yacht drifted closer and closer to the rocky shore and the breakers seemed dangerously close the crew donned their lifejackets, launched the dinghy and tried to reach the beach, clinging to the outside of it. But none of them reached the shore alive. The autopsy later showed that they died from concussion and head injuries. Drowning was secondary.

The yacht, however, survived. Though the main anchor was broken part of it wedged itself under a rock and held the yacht at a safe distance from the shore. Three days later, she was recovered and taken to her destination, Cannes, without as much as a scratch on her topsides. Nobody who saw her immaculate in her berth would ever have suspected that a few days before five people had died after abandoning her.

• • • • • • •

# Ghost stories

*Some of the yachts mentioned below fall into the category of boats which were abandoned but did not sink. The full story about some of the others, though perhaps less mysterious than that of the* Marie Celeste, *will never be known.*

For as long as ships have sailed the sea there have been sailors' superstitions. Some happenings at sea are hard to explain. Some phenomena, like *Fata Morgana*, have a scientific explanation. Others defy explanation of any kind.

The fate of some ships falls into the latter category. They include ships that have inexplicably vanished without trace and others that have been found sailing along perfectly normally, but with no one on board. No less mysterious than the case of the *Marie Celeste*, though less well known, is that of the *Sea Bird*.

## Sea Bird

It was a fine sunny day in 1750 on the coast near Newport, Rhode Island, with a good offshore breeze to speed the multitude of shipping on its way, when the inhabitants of Easton Beach were amazed to see a brig, instead of beating into Newport, sail straight for the sandbanks off their village. Was the captain crazy? The fishermen signalled to the vessel to change course but she sailed serenely on, straight up the beach on an even keel with all sails drawing. Now her name, *Sea Bird*, could be made out.

When they had got over their initial surprise people climbed on board. What they found was even more astonishing. In the galley a pot of coffee stood steaming on the stove. Breakfast was ready. Everything was neat and in good order. The log revealed nothing unusual. But there was no one on board. The only living thing was the ship's dog.

According to the log the brig was due in Newport that day. It was never established why the crew had apparently left the ship which sailed on by herself towards her next port of call.

In contrast, the reasons for modern yachts becoming ghost ships are often all too clear. In some cases a singlehanded skipper has fallen overboard and the yacht has sailed on, steered by her self-steering gear. In other cases boats have been abandoned by their crews to the questionable security of a liferaft or the risks of boarding a passing ship, or they have been lifted off by helicopter, leaving the yacht to her own devices.

## Connemara IV
When this yacht, registered in London, was found drifting 400 miles south of Bermuda in September 1955 without her crew she showed obvious signs of having been through two hurricanes as her log and charts confirmed. But she was still afloat and well equipped. The crew, however, must have left her days before, preferring the doubtful safety of the liferaft, and were never found.

## Little One
This is the smallest of the yachts listed here and the one that drifted for the longest time. She was only 11 ft 6 in (3.5 m) overall. Her owner was famous. Born in Hamburg in 1896, William Willis emigrated to the United States in 1909. He lived all his life on and by the sea and undertook many remarkable voyages, claiming, 'It is in my nature to attempt the impossible!'

He became world-famous in 1957 for crossing the Pacific from Callao in Peru to Pago Pago in Samoa, a distance of 6,700 miles, on a balsa raft made of seven logs appropriately named *The Seven Little Sisters*, covering a longer distance on a smaller raft than Thor Heyerdahl had on the legendary *Kon-Tiki* a few years before.

At the age of 74 Willis tried to cross the Atlantic alone in his miniature yacht *Little One*. He had to give up on 7 October 1967 after using up all his provisions. He had already covered two-thirds of the distance from the New to the Old World when he and his boat were taken aboard a Polish cargo ship.

On 1 May 1968, now aged 75, he tried once more to sail the Atlantic in this speck of a boat but he never reached the European coast. On 22 September a Russian ship found the dismasted boat 400 miles west of Ireland, identifying her by Willis's passport and documents found on board. Of the 150 days that had elapsed between her departure and the day she was found, Willis could not have been on board for much more than 60 days. *Little One*, however, had tried to sail on to Europe on her own. She nearly succeeded.

## Vagabond

Only five days into her voyage and with all sails drawing, the small Swedish yacht *Vagabond* was found sailing herself into the Atlantic. Her owner, the singlehanded sailor Peter Wallin, had left his home port of Kalmar on 1 May 1969 and sailed via Kiel to Plymouth. From here he departed at the end of June bound for the Azores. On 6 July the Swedish ship *Golar Frost* sighted the yacht. When nobody answered their call, some of the crew went across to the small sailing boat. They found a sound, well-equipped yacht with no one on board. The last entry in the log was dated 2 July. Peter Wallin must have fallen overboard and his boat became a ghost yacht.

## Stella Maris

Another ghost yacht was *Stella Maris* in which the 60-year-old singlehander John Pflieger had hoped to sail from Bermuda to Antigua in the summer of 1966. He was nothing less than the founder and long-serving secretary of the Slocum Society, the worldwide association of singlehanded yachtsmen. Everything was in perfect order on board, from the well-trimmed sails to the pipe on the saloon table, when she was found sailing along without him. On 10 July, Pflieger had chatted with the captain of a tanker on 20°26'N , 061°18'W, about 200 miles north of Antigua. Then, close to his destination, he disappeared.

## *Jessie W*

The trimaran *Jessie W* drifted for over 50 days in the Pacific with the dead body of her skipper on board. The Reverend Frederick Watts who only discovered his love for the sea as a pensioner was 82 years old when he left Suva in April 1969 on his last voyage. He had already had several heart attacks, suffered from cancer and knew that his days were numbered.

On 22 July a ship sighted the dismasted trimaran about halfway between Fiji and New Zealand. When a boat went across to the trimaran, the skipper's body was found. The last log entry was dated 29 May, more than 50 days earlier, and was just a standard record of course, wind and weather.

The boat had probably lost her mast after her skipper had already died. The captain of the ship decided to bury the sailor and his boat at sea. The sea cocks were opened and both sank into the dark blue depths of the Pacific Ocean.

## *Teignmouth Electron*

A strange case of a ghost yacht was *Teignmouth Electron* found on the morning of 10 July 1969 under full sail about 700 miles south-west of the Azores in position 33°11'N, 40°26'W in an area not frequented by yachts. The first mate of the freighter *Picardy en route* from England to the Caribbean tried to contact the yacht. When he received no response he alerted the captain, Richard Box. He circled the trimaran three times sounding the siren, which would have woken the dead at that distance.

As this still did not elicit any response from the trimaran whose homeport, Bridgewater, could be read on the stern, Box stopped the ship and sent a boat across. The first mate, Clark, boarded the yacht and confirmed that there was no one on board. The cabin gave the impression that she had only been abandoned moments before. Dirty dishes filled the sink and on the table lay a soldering iron and some parts of a radio which

*Donald Crowhurst on the foredeck of* Teignmouth
Electron.

someone obviously had been repairing. Clark also found the
log book open, the last entry being for 24 June. The last entry
in the radio log was for 29 June.

Apparently *Teignmouth Electron* had been sailing the
Atlantic with no one on board for over ten days. Somebody on
*Picardy* remembered the singlehanded round the world race
which was close to finishing at the time and thus identified
Donald Crowhurst as the missing sailor. The discovery of the
trimaran was reported to the shipowners and as the weather

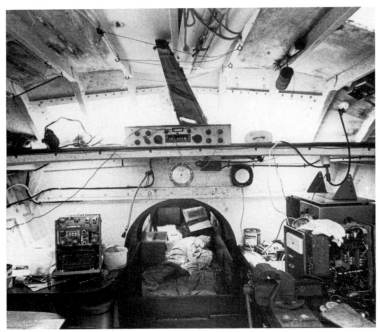

*The deserted cabin of* Teignmouth Electron *as she was discovered by the crew of the cargo ship* Picardy *on 10 July 1969.*

was calm she was hoisted on board the freighter. A full scale search for Crowhurst was launched in the area (see page 131).

There is not enough space here to detail the strange events that preceded *Teignmouth Electron*'s becoming a ghost yacht, aimlessly sailing the south Atlantic with Crowhurst reporting false positions over a long period. This was the story that first revealed itself to Box as he studied *Teignmouth Electron*'s double logs.

## *Southern Cross*

The small yacht *Southern Cross* ran aground on the American coast ten miles north-east of Cape May not far from the entrance to Delaware Bay on 2 November 1969. The 53-year-old singlehanded sailor George Sosman had left Long Island

Sound a few days before intending to visit his son at the naval academy at Annapolis. *Southern Cross* sailed a few days as a ghost yacht, crossing several busy shipping lanes in the approaches to New York and Philadelphia. How Sosman went overboard is not known.

## Frilo

Another ghost yacht was *Frilo* which the singlehander Chris Loehr intended to sail across the Atlantic by the trade wind route during the winter of 1971. Loehr fell overboard and was never seen again. *Frilo* was later found by a British ship still sailing along. The last entry in her log was dated 31 January and described heavy weather sailing.

## Seebär

On 25 June 1971 the singlehanded sailor Werner Zirpel abandoned his yacht on a return crossing from America to Europe. She had been dismasted earlier but Zirpel had erected a jury-rig under which he made good progress eastwards. When he went alongside the Norwegian ship *Golar Borg* in order to obtain fresh provisions he unfortunately injured his hand seriously. Any thought of sailing farther had to be abandoned together with the boat. Zirpel went aboard the ship leaving *Seebär* to fend for herself. She sailed on for another three weeks under her jury-rig until on 15 July she was picked up by the Dutch freighter *Loire Lloyd* in position 47°33'N, 19°27'W and later returned to her owner in Hamburg virtually undamaged!

## Njord

This 26 ft (8 m) cruising yacht showed greater powers of endurance than her crew, a young couple who abandoned her on 16 September 1972 half-way between the French coast and the Balearic islands. The small gaff cutter was found three days later by the English yachtsman Patrick Chilton who manoeuvred his own boat close enough to board the *Njord*. But his attempt to take the boat in tow failed. The yacht sailed on for another ten days until she was finally picked up by the Danish freighter *Peder Most*.

Remarkably, the positions where the crew were found in the liferaft and where the boat was found after 13 days were only 20 miles apart.

## Galloping Gael

On 28 June 1976, the 38 ft (11.5 m) yacht *Galloping Gael* was found deserted near the Newfoundland Banks. She belonged to the Canadian singlehanded yachtsman Mike Flanagan who had been competing in the 1976 OSTAR and had left England bound for the finish at Newport. Flanagan was married with several children. When the boat was found the mainsail was half set and it is assumed that he fell overboard while reefing.

## Le Steph

The dismasted 33 ft 6 in (10.2 m) cruising yacht *Le Steph* drifted across the Atlantic for 42 days in September 1978. Demoralized after several storms off Newfoundland in the course of which the boat was dismasted, the French crew of six had been taken off by the fishing vessel *Arin Fisher* while attempting to make their way back to Canada under engine. An attempt to tow the yacht was unsuccessful. She was left adrift in the autumn gales in the North Atlantic with her companionway open. She drifted for six weeks until she was about 1,000 miles off the Irish coast where she was sighted by the small German container ship *Contship Three*. Her captain, Klaus Baltzer, decided to take her in tow but after 24 hours she filled with water and sank. A sad end to a brave yacht.

## 1979 Fastnet Race

The 19 yachts that remained afloat after being abandoned in the Fastnet Race of 1979 may also be regarded as ghost yachts. Some, though not all, were dismasted. Most of them drifted around off the Irish coast for several days.

Some of the crews of *Trophy*, *Grimalkin* and *Ariadne* met a tragic death after taking to liferafts, though the yachts themselves stayed afloat and could later be towed into harbour. The other yachts that survived without their crews included:

| | |
|---|---|
| *Allamanda* | *Golden Apple of the Sun* |
| *Alvena* | *Gringo* |
| *Billy Bones* | *Gunslinger* |
| *Camargue* | *Polar Bear* |
| *Flashlight* | *Skidbladner* |
| *Gan* | *Tarantula* |

## Tour du Monde

The crews of the Fastnet Race yachts abandoned their yachts only when they were in dire straits. It is difficult to understand the crew who left their new vessel adrift in the Atlantic simply because of rudder failure. This was the case with the brand new 39 ft (11.95 m) *Tour du Monde* that was abandoned on 16 February 1980 after rudder failure and a tow lasting several hours behind the cargo ship *Reefer Knight* only a handful of miles from the harbour of Los Cristianos on Tenerife. Her skipper, who held all appropriate qualifications, became alarmed while the boat was under tow and ordered her to be abandoned even though they were already within sight of the sunny coastline. The boat then drifted with the trade winds for 12 days towards the Caribbean until she was picked up by a Polish ship which had no problem in hoisting her on board and delivering her to Kiel a week later. For this she earned well over £15,000 in salvage.

## Samos

No one knows what finally became of the 22 ton steel yacht *Samos*. She had left Ibiza on 24 December 1980 with an experienced husband and wife crew for a short hop to the Spanish mainland. Heavy weather came suddenly and unexpectedly and for three days they lay hove-to until they were somewhat reluctantly taken off by the Swedish ship *Terso*. The master of the ship ordered the warp of the yacht to be cut when the woman found herself in a potentially dangerous situation while boarding the ship. The boat was left adrift in position 36°35'N, 001°16.5'W.

## Vale

The 33 ft (10 m) cruising yacht *Vale* was found abandoned on 10 August 1981 in the Baltic Sea off Bornholm. The tragic events which must have preceded her discovery, but cannot now be reconstructed with any certainty, happened in the main holiday season. It was the first of several such cases in European waters about this time.

Seven miles off the Swedish coast the trawler *Mainland* sighted the German yacht drifting with sails flapping. The fishermen found nobody on board the yacht which showed no sign of damage or other dramatic occurrences.

According to the log, the crew of *Vale*, consisting of Friedrich Jordan (44) and his son Torald (10), left Bornholm on 8 August at 0900. The boat must have been adrift for less than 45 hours after the crew were lost, whatever befell them.

## Mirebel

This ghost yacht was a 30 ft (9 m) production cruising boat found drifting north-east of Bermuda on 18 June 1984 by the Russian container ship *Skulptor Zalkans*. As in other cases, there was no trace of the small boat's crew. The yacht was hoisted on deck and handed over to the German authorities on the return voyage.

It was some time before anyone connected the abandoned yacht with the six Americans picked up from a liferaft in the same area off Bermuda around 10 June.

It turned out that *Mirebel* had left Hampton Roads on 27 May bound for Bermuda. In heavy weather the following day the crew took to the liferaft and left *Mirebel* adrift. The boat drifted for a week before she was picked up, earning the Russians a handsome salvage fee.

## Maxi 68

A pilot boat was anchored on station near the Cordouan light off the Gironde estuary on 7 February 1983. Suddenly a yacht appeared through the haze sailing directly towards them. They narrowly avoided a collision when the boat did not respond to any of their visual or sound signals. When they eventually caught up with the yacht they found she was sailing by autopilot. She was a Maxi 68 registered nearby and her skipper often sailed singlehanded. It was another sad case of a lone sailor falling overboard.

## *Sea Jay*

It is hard to imagine oneself in the situation of someone who abandons a seaworthy yacht and stands on the deck of the ship that he has chosen as a refuge, watching it drift away. Often those involved cannot understand their own reasoning at the time when they rethink the situation days later.

Marianne Topjian gives a memorable description of the abandoning of the 36 ft (11 m) cruising yacht *Sea Jay* in April 1983 *en route* from Mexico to Florida, including the moment when her skipper, Charles Wilson, hesitated for a few seconds before taking the decisive step from the yacht on to the lowest rung of the ladder up the ship's side and climbing wearily towards an uncertain future. Decisions taken at a time of stress often appear in a different light as soon as the weather improves.

*Sea Jay* left Cozumel, Mexico, on 12 April 1983 bound for Florida. Before embarking on a circumnavigation there were some repairs and additions to be made in her home port. On the first day out from Mexico a burnt cable rendered the new engine useless. 'But as sailing yachts are made for sailing, we continued our voyage,' Topjian recalls.

For the next 48 hours *Sea Jay* performed well, but then the vane steering gear broke down. Wilson hung head-down over the stern for several hours in what had become a heavy swell to dismantle it. He was exhausted by this exercise but *Sea Jay*, now steered by hand, continued to make good progress. Soon, they were within 200 miles of their destination.

On the morning of 15 April, a coastguard vessel called *Sea Jay* and asked if they have sighted a boat in distress. 'We told the coastguard what bad shape we were in with no engine or self-steering gear and only a very limited amount of battery capacity left,' Topjian says, 'and all they did was to ask us to keep a lookout for another boat and assist them should we sight it!' But eventually the coastguard agreed to relay *Sea Jay*'s difficulties to their headquarters. Topjian wondered afterwards whether they could have asked the coastguard to repair the electrical system of the engine.

But is it impossible to sail without an engine? The following night *Sea Jay*'s crew seemed to believe it may be so. They sighted two ships and the couple were afraid of being run down by one of them. However, the situation was resolved when Wilson contacted one of them on VHF.

On 16 April the yacht encountered heavy weather. They tried to beat to windward under storm canvas but did not make any headway. The next morning they were fearful that the cross-trees might break and so they hove-to. The thought of drifting back south-westwards was not attractive but they feared a dismasting more, even though the mast and rigging were undamaged.

Then, for no clear reason, they called for assistance on VHF. The tanker *Gulf Supreme* immediately changed course and advised them to leave the boat. As the tanker could not manoeuvre alongside the yacht they got under way again and went alongside the tanker, sailing up to the towering side of the ship as if it were a jetty.

'Charles manoeuvred successfully alongside,' Topjian recalls. 'Then they threw us a line and eventually our personal things, the dog and afterwards myself were hoisted on deck. The captain was sorry that he had no gear to lift *Sea Jay* on deck as well. So Charles followed at last, hesitating, not really wanting to, he left our yacht and climbed up the long ladder to the deck of the tanker. It was with very heavy hearts indeed that we watched our yacht, our home, drift slowly away.'

Two days later Topjian and Wilson were ashore at Fort Lauderdale, Florida, not knowing what had become of their yacht in the meantime. She was found on 26 April after drifting for around ten days, 60 miles south-west of Tampa, Mexico. A ship from St Lucia had finally brought her into harbour. Topjian only hints at the ensuing legal battle over salvage and the return of the yacht to her owners which continued for many months.

## *Misty*

*Misty* became a ghost yacht under mysterious and tragic circumstances in the summer of 1982. Peter Evans from Worthing had her built along the lines of Blondie Hasler's *Jester*. In the 25 ft 9 in (7.85 m) boat he had sailed from England via the Azores to the Caribbean and back again. In July 1982, with his

German girlfriend as crew, Evans embarked on a voyage to Australia.

Sadly it ended in the Bay of Biscay. On 11 July the Polish cargo ship *Buran* sighted *Misty* at around 1700 in position 45°43'N, 014°21'W, around 270 miles north-west of Cape Finisterre. She had been dismasted in winds of force 11 and was firing red distress rockets. The Polish ship took Evans and his girlfriend on board. But as he stood on the deck of the ship Evans evidently regretted this decision and climbed back on to the small boat, disappearing below decks.

Was he looking for money and passports? Or did he want to ensure the safety of his girlfriend, but not abandon the yacht? No one knows the answers to these questions. The ship stood by the yacht for a whole day but Evans never reappeared on deck. Eventually *Buran* had to continue her voyage.

Nearly four weeks later another Polish ship, bound for Canada, sighted *Misty* in position 43°55'N, 016°35'W, about 150 miles away from the first encounter, but now with no one on board. This ship took her on board. The Canadian authorities refused permission to unload the boat as the incident had not taken place in Canadian waters. So *Misty* stayed on the deck of the ship which eventually returned to Poland. What became of her then we do not know.

## Escape

This 28 ft (8.5 m) yacht, sailing under the South African flag, left St George's, Bermuda, on her way to England on 24 May 1984. It was the floating home of Ivan and Beverly Hatley and their 13-month-old daughter, Joanne. They had bought the yacht a year before with the proceeds of the house they had sold in South Africa. The family had sailed from Cape Town to the Caribbean and Bermuda. Here Ivan's younger brother, Paul, joined them for the trip across the Atlantic via the Azores back home to England.

By 2 June *Escape* had covered about a third of the distance to the Azores when a depression caught up with them. At first the winds were south-easterly force 7 but the barometer kept falling and eventually the anemometer hit the end of its scale.

For the crew of *Escape* the only possibility was to lie a-hull and retire to the cabin. Sunday 3 June was passed in this fashion.

Just as they were welcoming a decrease in the wind the following day, it suddenly veered through 60° and started to blow again. A murderous cross sea soon developed which eventually capsized *Escape* and rolled her through 360°. Joanne was bombarded by food tins and it was a wonder that she remained uninjured. Both men received cuts and bruises. The yacht started to make water. The engine mounting bolts appeared to have sheared. The rudder was jammed. The mast was broken just above deck and now lay alongside, banging dangerously against the hull.

The men cut away the mast and rigging. But what now? Should they try to make the remainder of the 2,000 miles to Flores or call for help on the radio? The leak can be stopped. The engine can be made to run again and even the rudder can be repaired. Weather improves. But the Hatleys nevertheless decide to call for assistance.

Two ships, *Nandu Arrow* and *TFL Adams*, receive the yacht's call and are able to fix her position. The crew of *Escape* keep a lookout for the ships but first they sight another yacht. On 5 June around 2000 they see a yacht sailing towards them under storm sails. Ivan sets off an orange smoke signal to assist the other yacht which they assume is looking for them. But the other boat does not see the distress signal. Apparently they are not even keeping a lookout. As they pass, an estimated 1,000 yards away, the Hatleys can distinctly make out figures on the other's deck, hoisting sail and sailing away.

Ivan is distraught. He can't believe his eyes. How could the other yacht not have seen them? Angrily he starts the engine which fires up promptly and follows the disappearing yacht at full speed of just under 6 knots. The engine vibrates badly on its mountings. Navigation lights are switched on aboard the other yacht but as she still does not react even to red distress rockets Ivan gives up the chase.

An hour later the navigation lights of a ship appear over the horizon. Soon after, *Nandu Arrow* stops within shouting distance. Paul starts the engine and Ivan brings the yacht alongside the ship from which several lines are lowered.

*The skipper of* Mikado *removing equipment from the abandoned* Escape *in mid-ocean before scuttling her.*

Alongside the ship it is evident how high the swell still is; *Escape* rises and falls 13 ft (4 m).

Joanne is hoisted on board in a secured bag. The adults clamber up the ladder. Beverly has trouble and is nearly crushed between the yacht and the ship when she is thrown about a few times before finally making it to safety. The yacht is cut adrift with all her gear, a worthwhile target for any would-be salvors.

And the vultures are already closing in. The 56 ft (17 m) German-registered charter yacht *Mikado*, which only left Bermuda on 1 July, has made a fast passage along the same route to the Azores so far. The larger yacht has been able to keep on sailing throughout the gale. The crew have heard the radio conversation between *Escape* and her rescuers. They are not quite within sight of *Nandu Arrow* but they know the position of the incident.

At night on 6 July *Mikado*'s skipper, Knut, can see the ship in his radar. At 0300 he sights the *Escape*. Over the radio he asks the captain of *Nandu Arrow* for confirmation that the yacht is adrift, abandoned and thus legally without owner-ship. The crew of *Mikado* discuss among themselves whether they can tow *Escape* to Flores, but this plan is abandoned as the charter yacht has a schedule to keep and with another yacht in tow it would probably not be possible to do so.

But Knut has time enough to heave-to next to the other boat and loot her. He makes several trips in his inflatable dingy to the dismasted but otherwise undamaged yacht and removes anything of value. He even takes the trouble to take out all electronics and unbolt the winches from around the cockpit. The autopilot is also taken as are all sails and warps.

The looting goes on for nearly five hours. Afterwards *Escape* is little more than an empty shell and Knut opens the seacocks. He then reports to the shipping authorities that this 'danger to shipping' has been removed, much to the disadvantage of the Hatleys. It is hard to see how the yacht could have been described as a danger in the middle of the Atlantic.

## Eumel

A ghost yacht incident in coastal waters involved the 36 ft (11 m) cruising yacht *Eumel* which ran around on a sandbank near Kronsgård on the Danish side of the Flensburg fjord on 13 August 1984. The yacht was undamaged and still seaworthy but nobody was on board.

A couple of hours later it was established that the boat belonged to the Flensburg-based yachtsman Werner Jacob (46) who had left the harbour of Gelting Mole earlier on the same day under engine. He was alone on board and undoubtedly shared the fate of many singlehanded sailors, falling overboard and having his yacht sail away without him.

## Shanty

Another singlehanded yachtsman to take involuntary leave of his boat was Peter Pereira who was washed overboard from his dismasted yacht in the Atlantic roughly in position 48°N and 010°W during hurricane Hortensia on 4 October 1984. A passing ship took him on board but was not able to recover the yacht. *Shanty* drifted for ten days in the busy shipping lanes from Europe to Africa and South America before finally being towed into Porto by a Portuguese naval vessel. It was Pereira's good fortune that due to the good connections of his club,

Trans Ozean, he was contacted in Argentina when his boat arrived in Portugal. Eventually the yacht was returned to him and, after repairs, became a seagoing boat once more.

### Skarabäus

An incident of a singlehanded yachtsman falling overboard in the summer of 1985 also had a happy ending.

After going overboard, Egon Purkl saw his boat sailing away in fine style, leaving him in the Mediterranean, near the Liparian islands, wearing nothing but bathing trunks. He survived by swimming for 24 hours before he was spotted and saved. (His story is told on page 179.)

The yacht sailed on for another six days and was finally found by an Italian yachtsman off the north coast of Sicily. Purkl, whose papers, documents and money were still on board, was able to get his yacht back after paying about £1,300 salvage.

• • • • • • •

# *The Bermuda Triangle*

*The so-called 'Bermuda Triangle' includes some
of the best cruising waters in the world. Not
surprisingly, yachts occasionally come to grief
here and enthusiasts for the Triangle are quick to
claim them as evidence of a malignant force.
However, less sensational explanations can
usually be found.*

Not long ago the market for books about strange goings-on in the 'Bermuda Triangle' was booming. The corners of the triangle are generally defined as Bermuda in the north, Puerto Rico in the south, and Miami in the west. However, some authors extend the triangle almost as far as the Azores and take in much of the eastern seaboard of the United States as well as

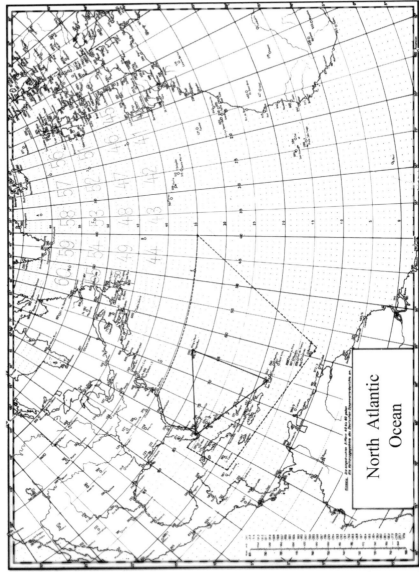

The Bermuda Triangle. Standard (solid line) and enlarged
version (broken line).

18–20 *The yacht* Christine II *is
salvaged with the aid of two large
rubber floats after running ashore
in darkness in the Lesser Antilles
and sustaining serious damage
below the waterline. She is towed
into harbour almost totally
submerged (18).*

21 The overturned motor cruiser Medusa *which came to rest almost out of the water after hitting the bank* of the Trave *at 25 knots.*

22 The yacht Arcona *driven ashore by a hurricane in the Virgin Islands. When she started to drag her anchor, her owner cut the warp to try and save*

23

23–25   *The catamaran* Gust *was damaged beyond repair by an onshore swell after being allowed to dry out on a beach in the Channel Islands in fair*

*The centreboarder*
Freizeit *after being
raised from the bottom
of the Minsener Rinne.
She ultimately became
a total loss when a sling
broke as she was being
craned ashore.*

27   *The singlehanded*
Black Beauty *was
caught on a lee shore
by a sudden autumn
gale on the
Mediterranean coast of
France. Unable to
make harbour or gain
sea room, she stranded
and sank in shallow
water not far from the
outer breakwater of
Port Gruissan.*

28  *The aftermath of a tropical cyclone in Tahiti. Cyclones are a hazard common to most of the world's exotic cruising grounds.*

29–31 *Fire is one of the worst nightmares for yachtsmen in both sailing craft and powerboats.*

**32–37** The brand new charter yacht *Arcadia came to grief in the Greek islands after dragging her anchor. Most of the damage, however, was caused by the well-intentioned efforts to salvage her.*

34

36

37

Barbados and Cuba, thereby including most of the Caribbean. This is, of course, a popular cruising ground and some of the victims claimed for the triangle have been yachts.

## Connemara IV

In September 1955 the London-registered yacht *Connemara IV* was found drifting about 400 miles south-west of Bermuda. She was quite badly damaged but still afloat. According to her log which was found aboard, she had sailed from New York on a southerly course that led her straight into the paths of two hurricanes, hurricane Connie and, a week later, hurricane Diane. These storms followed nearly identical paths with windspeeds in excess of 50 knots and claiming 100 lives.

In addition, two weeks later hurricane Ione must also have passed over the yacht. At some stage her crew must have left the badly damaged and apparently doomed yacht and taken to the liferaft. But while *Connemara IV* remained afloat her crew did not survive. Nothing was ever found of them.

## Revonoc

The case of the 43 ft (13 m) centreboard yawl *Revonoc*, which disappeared without a trace, is one of the most striking. The yacht was a modern well-founded ocean-going yacht owned and sailed by the one-time commodore of the Cruising Club of America, Harvey Conover (*Revonoc* is Conover spelt backwards). His crew, consisting of his wife, son and daughter-in-law as well as another offshore yachtsman, were equally experienced. They started their fateful journey from Key West to Miami on 1 January 1958.

The crew should have been well qualified to deal even with the 70 knot northerly winds which suddenly and without warning replaced the light south-easterlies. But anyone who has ever sailed in the Straits of Florida in a strong north wind which is blowing against a current of about 2 to 4 knots will know the particularly nasty short steep breaking seas which these conditions create. Even hove-to it is very difficult for a yacht to cope with this treacherous sea, unlike a yacht hove-to in the open ocean where wind and sea come from the same quarter and there is no current.

*Revonoc, a 43 ft (13 m) yawl with an experienced crew of five, disappeared without trace on a passage from Key West to Miami in January 1958.*

But Conover had already weathered a severe northerly in these waters two years previously on one of the first passages in his new yacht. In the magazine *Yachting* he wrote about the experience and the actions taken to weather the storm. He said, 'The waves reached mountainous heights during the night. But I felt that we would be able to withstand even more wind under our smallest storm sails, should the necessity arise or should we hit even worse weather. The seakeeping ability of *Revonoc* gave me the utmost feeling of security and I am sure that, with the right crew and the right decisions, we could even survive a full hurricane, provided there was enough sea room.'

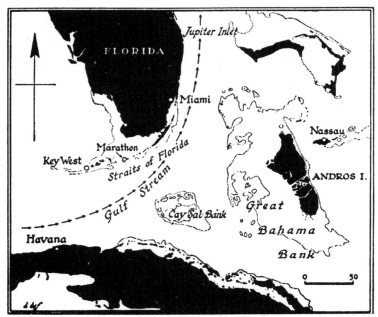

*Map showing the Straits of Florida where* Revonoc *disappeared. Her dinghy was later found at Jupiter Inlet.*

On her last voyage it would appear that *Revonoc* was well crewed and well skippered, and she had enough sea room as she sailed north.

When the well-known yacht did not arrive in Miami by 6 January, a big search operation was launched over a wide area. But it was, as the then editor of *Yachting*, William Taylor, remarked, 'like looking for the proverbial needle in the haystack. Yachts are so difficult to identify in the open sea, especially if they are disabled.' The search was indeed fruitless. *Revonoc* was never found.

The American yachting fraternity considered many possible explanations for the disaster. Eventually *Revonoc*'s dinghy was found virtually undamaged at Jupiter Inlet, north of Miami, but this did not shed any light on the disappearance of the yacht and her crew.

The general opinion was that the yacht with her experienced

crew would have survived the storm, but quite likely she was run down by a ship as she was fighting her way northward during the night close to the Florida coast. In the big seas and with the yacht well heeled over, her lights might possibly not have been visible to other ships. A fact supporting this thesis is that ships sailing south through the Straits of Florida hug the coast to avoid the main force of the north-setting Gulf Stream. On radar, the wooden-hulled *Revonoc* would have given only a poor echo, maybe none at all when hidden in the wave troughs. Moreover, ships operated under flags of convenience may not keep a proper lookout or radar watch. Finally, with large ships like oil tankers in the vicinity there was a risk not only of being run down but also, if the yacht was hove-to, of being sucked into the propeller where she would have been chopped to pieces.

'As regrettable as this tragic incident is,' wrote Taylor, 'it is also the fact that there really is nothing that we can learn from it to increase the safety of yachtsmen at sea.'

## *El Gato*

The yacht-broker Jan Bragg from Fort Lauderdale was an experienced yachtsman who had made several ocean voyages on his yacht *Fiddler's Green*. So it was nothing exceptional when he left Florida singlehanded to deliver the well-equipped 45 ft (13.7 m) yacht *El Gato* in several short hops via the Bahamas to Puerto Rico in October 1965.

*El Gato* and her one-man crew did indeed visit several Bahamian islands. On the leg from Exuma to the island of Great Inagua, however, she disappeared. Despite a long and intensive search by the coastguard in southern Bahamian waters, neither the yacht nor any wreckage from her was ever found.

Though the wind was strong at the time with seas of 16 to 20 ft (5 to 6 m), I think it is quite probable that *El Gato* was the victim of the very heavy traffic in this area where ships bound for the Panama Canal from Europe and North America are funnelled through the passage between Cuba and Hispaniola. Bragg was alone on board and had to sleep some-time.

## *Donald Crowhurst's* Teignmouth Electron *yields four other ghost yachts*

When Donald Crowhurst on the last leg of his supposed circumnavigation failed to make a scheduled radio call, a large scale search for him was instigated across the entire Atlantic.

If a yacht is reported missing, most ships will keep a better lookout in the relevant area than usual. This is even more the case when the missing yachtsman is a well-known singlehanded sailor who is apparently nearing the end of a circumnavigation that has lasted several months and is the probable winner of a substantial sum of money. So it is little wonder that, though *Teignmouth Electron* was not found immediately, at least four other yachts were found in the area between Bermuda and the Azores within a week.

The *Picardy* found the trimaran under full sail on 10 July 1969 about 700 miles south-west of the Azores with her equipment intact including two liferafts, but without her skipper. The last log entry was dated 24 June and there were no signs of any emergency so it is assumed that Donald Crowhurst fell overboard and drowned.

In the course of the same search the cargo ship *Maple Bank* sighted the white hulls of a 60 ft (18 m) catamaran on 1 July, drifting keel-up 300 miles north-east of Bermuda. No survivors were found.

On 6 July the cargo ship *Golar Frost* found the small Swedish sailing cruiser *Vaga* which had sailed under full sail across the Atlantic with no one on board. The captain sent a party across to the boat who established that it belonged to the Swedish singlehanded yachtsman Peter Wallin whose last log entry was dated 2 July. The boat was in good order, sailing well and completely undamaged. The owner is assumed to have fallen overboard and drowned.

On 4 July the steamer *Cotopaxi* sighted a 33 ft (10 m) cruising yacht on an easterly course apparently unmanned. The ship let the yacht sail past without attempting to board her.

On 8 July the tanker *Helisoma* sighted a capsized yacht, probably a multihull, of around 36 ft (11 m) in length between the Azores and the Portuguese coast. The captain of the tanker reported the drifting yacht as a 'danger to shipping'.

These encounters raise several points including the following:

- If a better watch were kept by ships in mid-ocean, the risk for yachts of being run down could be reduced.
- There are more half-sunk or capsized yachts floating around the oceans and representing a potential danger to other craft than yachtsmen may care to admit.
- Singlehanded sailing is a dangerous sport. The single-handed yachtsman is especially vulnerable when asleep. And if he falls overboard he is almost certainly doomed.

## Ixtapa

On 25 December 1971 the 52 ft (16 m) motorsailer *Ixtapa* left one of the southern entrances of the Intracoastal Waterway off Florida to sail to Key West along the coast. The boat was crewed by her owner and three friends.

When they had not arrived several days later despite the fair weather, the Coast Guard started a search. Shortly afterwards, several pieces of *Ixtapa*'s coachroof were found in the sea but no further wreckage. There were no signs of a fire or explosion so it was assumed that the boat was run down by a ship in the busy Straits of Florida.

## The lucky escape of Talmadge Riggens

It was a combination of luck and a sharp lookout on the radar that enabled Talmadge Riggens and his crew to escape a collision with a tanker in a mere 20 ft (6 m) long boat after the engine had failed off the Florida Keys and she had drifted out into the shipping lanes in February 1972.

'We were nearly run down by a tanker, whose watch shone a searchlight at us,' Riggens reported. 'They did not react to our shouting and waving our arms to show we were in distress. They must have thought it was a bizarre greeting or maybe anger. Anyway she disappeared leaving us wallowing in her wake.'

They were lucky. They could easily have been run down and obliterated like so many other boats and their crews.

## Saba Bank

The large offshore cruising yacht *Saba Bank* left Nassau on the Bahamas, manned by her skipper Cy Centner and a crew of three on 10 March 1974. The boat was to be tested on a shake-down cruise at the end of which the crew intended to sail to Miami. The skipper had allowed three weeks for the whole trip.

But at the end of three weeks the yacht did not arrive in port. When there still was no sign of her a few days later the Coast Guard started a search. But nobody had seen or heard anything of her and after a while she was officially listed as missing.

Although the Straits of Florida can sometimes be a rough and dangerous area when the wind blows against the Gulf Stream and a high sea develops, it seems more probable that this yacht was another victim of the large volume of shipping in this part of the world.

# 5

# THE RESCUERS

## *Unwanted assistance*

*Seafarers are sometimes accused of not helping others in distress, but in this case the crew of an oil tanker proceeded to rescue a yachtsman and his yacht even though he didn't seem too keen on being rescued!*

J Neuhaus was an officer of a tanker of 125,000 gross registered tons with a length of 869 ft (265 m), a beam of 128 ft (39 m) and decks which are 72 ft (21.8 m) above sea level. In the spring of 1985 the ship was in ballast and on its way from Europe to Tenerife. Neuhaus was on watch and saw a light off the starboard bow at 0700 one morning which he believed could be a distress signal. 'As the signal was only very short we had no time to take a bearing but changed course in the estimated direction,' said Neuhaus.

The distance to the supposed signal was seven miles. After ten minutes he could see tiny blips on the radar from time to time at intervals of about ten minutes 'which moved south-west with appreciable speed'.

So the vessel on the radar was actually sailing like the tanker towards the Canary Islands. It might have seemed unlikely that a yacht making good speed before a fresh north-easterly breeze was in distress and the same thought seems to have occurred to Neuhaus. 'When we had closed to about three miles we could see that it was a sailing boat running before the wind under genoa which did not seem unusual under the circumstances.'

Neuhaus then tried to contact the yacht by signal lamp but there was no reaction. Still not surprising if everything was well on board. Anyway, very few yachts carry signal lamps. Possibly the tanker's signals were not noticed on the yacht. She had self-steering gear and so there may have been nobody on deck at the time. However, these possibilities seem not to have been considered by Neuhaus.

'When we finally closed to about one-and-a-half miles the yacht lowered her genoa,' continues Neuhaus. At this point the tanker was ten lengths away. 'That was the only reaction to our approach and our signals. Many of my colleagues would by now have turned away from the yacht in irritation.' Perhaps Neuhaus should have done the same? If the yacht had wanted something from the tanker surely someone would have signalled by now.

The yacht was the *Yomider*, 25 ft 3 in (7.7 m) long, in which a French singlehanded yachtsman was on his way to the Canaries.

What does one do if in the middle of the ocean a giant tanker comes dangerously close and stops alongside? Perhaps they are just taking photographs. Perhaps they have a present for you. How does one feel with an acre and a half (6000 m²) of steel looming up close by? In such a situation most people would probably, somewhat apprehensively, await further developments.

For the next few minutes nothing happened. Both parties stared at each other. No one waved. Many pairs of eyes looked down at the small yacht and the yachtsman calmly looked back.

'We noticed that the rudder blade was lying in the cockpit. Now we were sure that the yacht needed assistance. But the solo skipper just sat motionless on the coachroof, where he had seated himself after lowering the sail, and looked at us.'

The yacht was a Fantasia designed by Philippe Harlé, a small trailable cruising yacht with a transom-hung rudder that can be easily removed for road transport. Possibly the owner had only taken it into the cockpit for minor repairs. Even if the damage was more substantial it would have been comparatively simple to rig a jury rudder on the transom, possibly using the original rudder blade and the existing mountings. The small lightweight yacht could also have been kept on course downwind by lines streamed from either side of her wide transom. Or perhaps the foresail itself would have done it, after all, the boat was sailing along smartly before the tanker made her appearance. In the trade winds, the course to the Canary Islands would have been a continuous broad reach.

From the point of view of the skipper who was still sitting impassively, waiting for whatever might be in store for him, there was no reason whatsoever for the tanker to stop next to him and offer unwanted assistance. The flash of light that had been the reason for the tanker changing course towards the

*The French yacht* Yomider *alongside the supertanker which came to her assistance.*

yacht might just have been a reflection of the sun which had by chance been observed on the bridge of the tanker.

So far the yachtsman had not indicated any desire for assistance, let alone salvage. On the other hand, Neuhaus for some reason still believed that he wanted help and criticizes him for his inactivity. 'If someone is in distress and wants to be rescued he should of course prepare the boat as much as possible and at least have lines, fenders and boathook at the ready.' If, on the other hand, he does not prepare the boat one might assume that he just does not need or want any help. What Neuhaus criticizes could actually just have been a reasonable reaction by the yachtsman.

'Manoeuvring close to the yacht was not easy and took a while. Unfortunately, the yachtsman had still not got himself or his boat ready for rescue. He was unable to pick up the lines that were thrown to him and fell into the water close to the boat as he did not have a boathook to hand. We had to manoeuvre into position again and even this attempt nearly failed for the same reasons. When he finally grabbed a line there was not enough time to attach a stronger warp to it.'

The whole episode must have seemed more and more bizarre to the Frenchman. Perhaps he had hoped to have a crate of beer or fresh bread lowered down to him on one of the lines. Ships had even been known to offer yachtsmen a hot bath.

But the ship's officers several storeys above the yacht carried on regardless. 'On the heaving line we passed a thick warp down to the yacht which was belayed to the mast. When at last we had the yacht alongside and under the crane it became obvious that the yachtsman did not even know how to fasten the lifting straps around the hull. Eventually the boatswain had to board the yacht and attach the straps. The yacht was then finally hoisted on deck. The whole operation had taken five hours.'

The yachtsman and his yacht remained on the tanker until Tenerife. Presumably he used the opportunity to repair the rudder. Just off the coast *Yomider* was launched again.

How the Frenchman reacted to this forcible rescue is unfortunately unknown but Neuhaus persisted in his view of the incident and offered the following advice to yachtsmen:

Yomider *is lifted on to the deck of the supertanker at the
end of a five hour operation.*

- Never assume that the ship has actually seen your distress signals.
- When a ship approaches signal clearly that the yacht is in distress, for example by the flag signal 'NC' or by transmitting 'SOS' with a powerful flashlight or with a mirror by day.

But corresponding advice might also be offered to Neuhaus by yachtsmen:

- Do not assume that the other vessel is in distress in the absence of a signal.
- When approaching a yacht under sail do not attempt to render assistance unless the crew signal that assistance is required.
- If no signal is forthcoming don't commence rescue operations unless the yacht is clearly abandoned or the crew are unable to cope by themselves.
- If closing with a yacht at sea, a large ship should not get so close as to appear to threaten her with damage or being run down.

While applauding the willingness of a professional seaman to help a yacht at sea, one may ask why there could be no communication between the vessels, if only by shouting, if there was no VHF on the yacht? Was the language barrier insuperable? Was it too far to shout? Was there too much other noise? Was there no way to communicate at all, even using sign language?

I do not know how I would have tried to fend off such a determined rescue effort, especially if verbal communication was impossible and sign language might have been misunderstood. I might have hoisted a 'Q' flag which every yacht has on board when cruising foreign waters, meaning 'Everyone is healthy on board. I request free practique'.

I wonder how Neuhaus would have interpreted this signal.

• • • • • • •

# Chichester's last transatlantic race

*After retiring from the 1972 singlehanded transatlantic race, Sir Francis Chichester's* Gipsy Moth V *was rammed by a ship which mistakenly thought he might be in need of assistance. The incident had a tragic sequel next day when the same ship rammed and sank another yacht with the loss of seven lives.*

No one outside his family knew that the famous yachtsman was suffering from cancer and had only a few months to live when he started in the 1972 singlehanded transatlantic race. The well-proven *Gipsy Moth V* had been equipped with radio so that Chichester could keep in direct contact with his family. When he started as one of 52 participants on 18 June 1972 his aim was to reach the finish; winning was out of the question, competing in his old yacht against purpose-built racing machines sailed by strong fit sailing professionals, hungry for victory.

Chichester decided to take the southern route across the Atlantic. On the second day out and quite untypically for the time of year, a depression with strong winds and low visibility swept over the fleet. Several competitors ran into trouble and had to retire. Chichester weathered this patch of bad weather but it cost him much strength and he felt very unwell.

He treated himself with the medicines which he had on board but primarily, he was worried by the fact that from the outset the radio did not work. While he could receive with it, it would not transmit at all. This was particularly irritating as he could listen to the more and more urgent messages from his family, asking him to answer their calls, but was obliged to remain silent. Try as he might, it was not possible to repair the set at sea. Naturally, his family and people ashore started to be concerned about him.

Meanwhile, *Gipsy Moth* sailed on, with a south-westerly course bound for warmer regions in which to cross the

Atlantic. Chichester followed his doctor's advice and rested as much as he could, at least ten minutes in every hour, lying on a cushion in the cockpit.

After six days of enforced radio silence during which his family's anxiety grew and some radio news bulletins openly speculated about his whereabouts and wellbeing, the 71-year-old skipper suffered a mental and physical breakdown. The medication had numbed his senses and when he finally regained consciousness he could not tell for how long he had blacked out – one night or maybe even two. But he was alert enough to make a sensible if not easy decision. His health obviously would not allow him to fulfil his ambition and carry on across the Atlantic. So he turned the boat round and headed back towards England on 25 June.

Sailing back towards the English Channel, Chichester's condition did not improve. By now very weak, he was worried at the prospect of having to enter the Channel with its busy shipping lanes where he would have to keep an almost continuous lookout. He hoped to find some means of contacting his son, Giles, who could then join him on *Gipsy Moth* by boat or helicopter. But it would be some time before the boat was in the Western Approaches and *Gipsy Moth* sailed on.

It proved to be an unlucky encounter when on 27 June the cargo ship *Barrister* sighted *Gipsy Moth* half-way between the Azores and England and relayed her position to Lloyd's. The captain passed on the following message. 'After we gave a signal on our siren Sir Francis came on deck. He waved to us, then went to the self-steering gear at the stern of the boat apparently to make some adjustment. There was no sign of any emergency or distress situation. But as we circled the yacht there was no communication, either by radio or voice. But Chichester obviously needed no help. The yacht was in good condition, sailing under jib and mizen on a course of about 200°.'

John Anderson, an old friend of Chichester, and Giles Chichester were troubled by this report. *Gipsy Moth* had been sighted in a position not far from the British Isles at a time, ten days after the start, when she should have covered at least twice the distance towards America. She was thus very far behind the rest of the fleet and it was feared that Chichester's health, which might have been responsible for the delay, might have deteriorated sharply. Evidently he was still in the race as the ship had reported him to be steering a course of 200°.

In fact *Gipsy Moth* had not been on this course before the ship appeared. Chichester was already on his way home. Unfortunately this was not known on the ship.

At least his position was now known and it was easy for aircraft to monitor his progress. The press concentrated their attention on *Gipsy Moth*, speculating about his condition.

On 28 June an RAF Nimrod circled the yacht and communicated with him in Morse code. 'Are you OK?' it signalled.

Some minutes later Chichester replied, 'I was ill.'

'Do you require help?'

Chichester replied, 'I am well. No assistance required.'

Another plane flew out on the following day, 29 June. Again a conversation in Morse code took place, a long and difficult business. Chichester concluded with the message, 'I want to meet my son and Anderson in the English Channel.'

While a sentence like this is easily written and read, in Morse code it is not quite as straightforward. It consists of 12 words or 46 letters and as each letter is made up of several long or short flashes, Chichester had to send over a hundred flashes to the aircraft to transmit this simple sentence. For the purpose he had to wedge himself securely in place between the mast and the lower shrouds and aim his signal lamp continuously at the circling plane. If the aircraft was in the wrong place he had to stop signalling. And of course he could not be sure that all his signals would be interpreted correctly.

So it is not surprising that this Morse conversation on 29 June lasted for one-and-a-half hours, after which Chichester signalled, 'Weak and cold. Want rest,' and retired to the cabin.

The pilot attached more significance to the last message than Chichester intended. Next morning the English papers carried headlines like 'Chichester at the end of his strength'.

The Chichester family were also led to believe that he wanted to put into Brest. The pilots had read 'Want rest' as 'Want Brest' and this misunderstanding had dramatic consequences for *Gipsy Moth* which meanwhile sailed on northwards with Chichester still reasonably fit.

At noon on 30 June the French weather ship *France II* arrived at Chichester's position. She came extremely close to the yacht and prompted Chichester to signal the following message to her. 'I am well. I need no help. Please stand off.'

Chichester assumed that the French ship would have understood him. He tacked and went below to rest and eat after an exhausting morning. A quarter of an hour later a loud siren startled him and made him rush back on deck. He was astounded to see the bows of the French ship looming over his stern at a distance of less than 20 yards.

Chichester ran to the stern, attempting to disconnect the self-steering gear and steer clear of the ship. But there was not time and *France II* came even closer. 'I must know where you are heading for,' Chichester heard from above as the ship drew closer. Then the bows of *France II* rammed the stern of the yacht and scraped along the side, breaking the 46 ft (14 m) high mizzenmast half-way up.

Shortly afterwards an inflatable dinghy came up to *Gipsy Moth*. A man in the dinghy asked him, 'Do you need a doctor?'

Chichester was quick-witted enough to reply, 'I don't, but my boat does!' gesturing towards the broken mizzenmast. But the Frenchman did not understand and returned to his ship. A few minutes later *France II* steamed off and disappeared over the horizon.

As the mizzensail filled the top half of the mast snapped off and was left dangling between the masts, held aloft by the main backstay, thus endangering the mainmast as well. Chichester suffered badly from the unscheduled hard work of clearing the rigging and making the mainmast secure.

Meanwhile Giles Chichester and John Anderson chartered a helicopter that flew them out to the Royal Navy frigate *Salisbury* that had been ordered to intercept *Gipsy Moth* and offer assistance. The two vessels met 250 miles west of the English Channel. Together with three other yachtsmen from the Navy, Chichester and Anderson were put on board *Gipsy Moth*. They made repairs to the mast and rigging in the course of which one of the men had to go to the top of the mainmast, a dangerous task in mid-Atlantic, to disconnect the stay still holding the broken mast aloft. Then the new crew sailed the yacht back to Plymouth with Sir Francis resting below decks. It must be said that despite all his problems he would very probably have managed to sail the yacht back by himself eventually if there had been no alternative. Complaints in the British press, for example that the sorties of the Nimrod aircraft and the operation of the frigate had cost the taxpayer too much money, left him unperturbed.

It was harder to ignore the further havoc caused by *France II* after the ship had left him with a broken mizzen in the mid-Atlantic. Only about 12 hours later, just after midnight on 1 July, she ran down the American yacht *Lefteria* in the Bay of Biscay, killing seven members of the total crew of eleven. The four survivors were picked up by the ship and reached La Rochelle on the evening of 2 July.

The two American skippers, still in shock after both losing their wives in this appalling accident, had not yet made any statement when Associated Press released the following news item across the world, without even knowing where *Lefteria* had come from nor where she had been bound for: 'An official hearing was opened today into the collision of the French ship *France II* with the American yacht *Lefteria*. Both vessels were on their way to help the British singlehanded sailor Sir Francis Chichester who had fallen seriously ill while competing in the Singlehanded Transatlantic Race.'

Obviously this item attracted wide publicity and comment. The overwhelming majority of papers directly or indirectly blamed Chichester for the death of the Americans. Thus the veteran yachtsman had to fight hard in the last remaining six weeks of his life to clear his name from these unfounded allegations. Luckily not only his friends supported him but also the survivors of the *Lefteria* and, in the end, even the French minister of transport declared Chichester free from all blame in the incident. That was on 17 August 1972, just a few days before Sir Francis's death on 26 August.

His own regrets about the tragic accident of *Lefteria* were published in *The Times* on 8 July, even before the American skippers had had the opportunity to tell the world what had really happened.

*Lefteria* was an 80-year-old converted gaff schooner that

had originally been a Baltic trader. Her skipper, Philip Bates, had bought the boat together with his friend Peter Gallagher and rebuilt and re-equipped her over the course of a year in Denmark, intending to use her for chartering in the Caribbean. In June 1972 they had left Denmark and sailed via the English Channel to the Bay of Biscay with a crew of eleven that included the wives of the two owners.

*Lefteria* was sailing south when the watch saw the lights of a big ship bearing down upon them from dead astern at around 0100. The ship was *France II* which passed the schooner on her starboard side. Bates shone a searchlight at her and tried to communicate in Morse, probably to check his position, but received no intelligible reply. The ship held her course and when she was safely ahead Bates went below to the chart table. He had been there for less than two minutes when the schooner was hit amidships by *France II*, heeling her on to her beam ends. Bates was able to reach the deck before he was washed overboard. The schooner sank within seconds, leaving no chance of survival for most of her crew – the two wives, three young Americans, a Canadian and a Swede. Only four survivors were picked up by *France II*.

In a personal letter Bates confirmed to the ailing skipper of *Gipsy Moth* that he had heard of her neither before nor during the fateful voyage of *Lefteria* and that he had also known nothing about Chichester or his illness. Consequently it would have been impossible for him to have been heading towards *Gipsy Moth* in an attempt to help.

• • • • • • •

# The taxpayer to the rescue

*When the ultra-light trimaran* Yaksha *sank in mid-Atlantic during the 1969 OSTAR it precipitated a massive air and sea search for her solo skipper. The scale of the operation raised questions about the cost to the general public of such races.*

In the days before radio a ship's crew had to take care of themselves at sea and in the case of distress had to try and reach land by their own resources in a lifeboat or wait, sometimes for very long periods of time, to be picked up by another ship passing them by sheer chance. Yachtsmen exercised extreme caution. Ocean voyages were undertaken only in proven seaworthy craft. There was no reliance on rescue services and the first rule of seamanship was prudence.

Today yachts have less to fear. Satellite rescue systems allow continuous monitoring of all corners of the oceans. With an EPIRB any yacht can avail itself of rescue services automatically anywhere in the world. Wherever disaster may strike, the position of the yacht is known almost instantaneously and ships, aircraft or helicopters can be sent to the rescue.

The global rescue network can of course be misused. This is a particular issue in the growing sport of long-distance ocean racing where the quest for new challenges has led to some costly rescue operations. Obviously, aircraft and helicopters are expensive to run and ships diverted to the rescue lose time and money.

For this reason the media in some maritime countries are asking whether there is a limit to spending on large-scale rescue operations. In some countries, controversial safety regulations are applied to offshore cruising yachts (as in New Zealand) in an attempt to limit rescue costs. This discussion is, as we shall see, not new. The awkward question of how much we can afford to spend on saving a human life at sea was put for the first time after a rescue operation during the 1969

147

OSTAR in which 35 boats started in Plymouth bound for the finish off Newport. There were 22 monohulls and 13 multihulls.

The 49 ft (15 m) trimaran *Yaksha* sailed by the Frenchman Jean de Kat was not only the largest but also one of the lightest boats in the race, displacing a mere two-and-a-half tons. Only a few days into the race the multihull proved unequal to the harsh environment of the North Atlantic. A civil aircraft heard the distress call and passed it on, with a position of 54°N and 030°W, to the control centre at Prestwick. The message read, 'Lost rudder, mast and one hull. Boat is sinking. Am abandoning ship. This will be my last transmission.' The following rescue operation ensued.

*0804* The first Shackleton search aircraft takes off from Ireland.

*0830* Prestwick control centre broadcasts the information that the cargo ship *Irish Rowan* in position 55°54'N, 026°6'W is nearest to the scene. Details are passed on to the coastguard. *Irish Rowan* is requested to help the search.

*0845* The North Atlantic rescue coordination centre requests the weather ship *Charly* to head for the north-eastern limit of its area and stand by for further developments.

*0955* The US Air Force is asked to join in the search with an aircraft from the base at Keflavik, Iceland.

*1000* The steamship *Alice Bouwater* reports that she will be in the search area at 0800 on the following morning.

*1035* The sponsor and organizer of the race, *The Observer* newspaper, is contacted by telephone for more information and the previous course of the trimaran *Yaksha*.

*1043* The US Air Force base in Keflavik reports that their aircraft will be ready for takeoff at 1230.

*1142* The *Irish Rowan* is requested to continue the search.

*1300* The search area around is now being patrolled by several aircraft.

That afternoon two British and two American aircraft are in the area and at least four ships are on their way. The wind has risen to force 5 and the sea is streaked with whitecaps which does not help the search. There is low cloud so the aircraft have to fly low. Parachutes would be useless at this height. The search operation becomes potentially dangerous for the air crews.

*19 June, about 0900* The search aircraft 'Playmate 16' has engine problems after searching the area for eight hours. One engine has failed. The pilot radios that he is returning to Shannon.

*1115* 'Playmate 16' lands safely in Ireland. The pilot remarks that the search for one man might have cost ten lives if they had crashed.

*1330* A replacement aircraft takes off. The search continues for the remainder of the day, employing four aircraft and four ships.

*20 June* The control centre extends the area of the search to the south and east.

*1635* Some red plastic buoys are sighted in the sea. It turns out that they are of unknown origin and not connected to the *Yaksha*.

*1700* The search continues, the aircraft and ships giving hourly reports of their positions.

*1840* Almost exactly 60 hours after the start of the search operation 'Playmate 18' sights the missing yachtsman in position 53°55'N, 023°45'W. He is in a small inflatable dinghy and fires a red flare. While the aircraft circles above him the coastguard requests a sea state report.

*2100* A second aircraft drops a new dinghy with provisions, water and cigarettes. De Kat boards the new dinghy. From the aircraft he appears fit and well.

*2130* The Shackleton drops radio beacons and visual signals. Both aircraft circle above the casualty and transmit his position. Two ships change course towards the yachtsman.

*21 June, 0830* The Norwegian cargo ship *Jagona en route* from Canada to the Baltic is nearing the scene as is the American naval vessel *Dutlin*, a few miles further away.

*1145 Jagona* radios all ships, 'Have found and recovered missing yachtsman. He is fit and well.'

Despite all the concentrated effort of a coordinated search operation de Kat's rescue was still partly a matter of luck, over 70 hours after his boat went down. The Shackleton had already abandoned the search and was on its way back to base when one of the crew of ten by pure chance looked out of a window and spotted the orange dinghy in the sea below. Despite all the technology it was the 'Device: eyeball. Type: human. Version: open', as the Royal Air Force later put it in a statement, which finally brought the search to a successful end. Other searches on a similar scale, for example for Alain Colas and his boat *Manureva* during another singlehanded transatlantic race, were less successful.

Critical comments followed in the media, ranging from saying that de Kat was lucky to have been rescued to declaring that the cost of the rescue had been too high. For days sums varying between £50,000 and £250,000 were bandied about as the alleged cost of the search operation. Of course, it was noted that the taxpayer would have to pick up the bill.

In a television interview recorded when de Kat stumbled ashore for the first time after his ordeal and was still too shaken to form simple sentences, the rescued yachtsman was asked point-blank if his life was really worth £250,000. Not surprisingly he was too embarrassed to answer.

# 6
# SALVAGE STORIES

## At what cost?

*When the yacht* Yin & Yang *struck a coral reef in mid-Pacific the cost of salvage consumed almost the whole sum for which she was insured, leaving too little to pay for repairs. Demmy, on the other hand, was not insured at all and yet the owner managed to save her by a gruelling do-it-yourself salvage operation that took nearly five months.*

The object of navigation is to arrive safely at your destination; everything else is secondary. By 'everything else' I mean the various navigational errors that are apt to occur on any passage, such as steering an inaccurate course, poor fixes, mistaking or neglecting to establish your position, failing to notice or take account of tidal streams, incorrect identification of lights, and so on.

In busy, well-buoyed waters near home, where navigation is sometimes just a matter of following the shipping lanes, such navigational errors are seldom life-threatening. And in the event of trouble rescue is normally close at hand. But in more remote parts of the world the same errors, which any navigator can make despite meticulous chartwork, may lead to disaster. The risk is the price of crossing oceans and visiting exotic cruising grounds.

For example, the German 36 ft (11 m) steel sloop *Yin & Yang* ran aground on the uninhabited Tuamotu atoll, Ahunui, on 24 February 1982. The crew consisted of the owners, Axel and Julia Frühbuss, and their eight-year-old son, Fabian. The boat was insured, but after salvage the family was left with just an uninhabitable wreck.

It was dark as *Yin & Yang* ran towards the outer reef of Ahunui at high speed under full sail. The reef which completely encircled the paradisiacal lagoon inside lay directly in the path of the yacht, about 500 miles east-south-east of Tahiti. The yacht had neither radar nor GPS. Navigation among the nearly 100 atolls in the Tuamotus is extremely difficult as there are virtually no lights or radio beacons in the 1,000 mile long archipelago.

Once she had struck the reef the seas quickly pushed the steel yacht further and further on to the corals. Breakers had ripped the rudder off even before the skipper could take his wife and child to safety on the nearby uninhabited island. He then transferred water, food and all the equipment ashore that might be necessary for a Robinson Crusoe existence that could well last for months.

However, the stranded sailors were soon saved. Using the undamaged ham radio, Axel Frühbuss sent out a MAYDAY message the following morning which was received by an amateur radio operator on Tahiti. He alerted the harbour and naval authorities in Papeete who in turn ordered the nearby marine biological research vessel *Marara* to rescue the family from their atoll.

Obviously it is not easy for an insurance company to deal with a claim for total loss made from a distant tropical island. But it is in exactly this kind of situation than an owner will discover how reliable and trustworthy his insurers are. It seemed highly unsatisfactory from the point of view of both parties to attempt salvage, but that was the instruction received from the distant offices of the insurance company notwithstanding the fact that the salvage tug was stationed 500 miles away from the yacht.

The Berlin-based insurers of *Yin & Yang* maintained their insistence on salvage throughout a heated telex and telephone discussion lasting 30 days. In those four weeks following the stranding the yacht was, of course, lifted up by the waves and dropped back on to the coral many thousands of times.

It was a sorry sight that met the crew of the salvage tug *Aito* when they finally arrived at the scene of the stranding after steaming for 50 hours. The keel of the yacht was trapped by the coral and, with mast still standing, she was alternately being pushed over on to her side by the breakers and righting herself again. The hull on that side had been pushed in over a length of 13 ft (4 m). Under water there were several long cracks through which water was entering.

It was not easy for the salvage crew to reach the yacht with their inflatable dinghy. They then had to destroy the interior in order to fill the cabin with inflatable buoyancy bags. With her second hawser *Aito's* 1,200 hp finally dragged *Yin & Yang* free of the coral. Using a fothering sail and two motor-driven pumps they were able to tow the yacht for three days to Tahiti. What was then lifted out of the water and put ashore by a crane was nothing but a rusty wreck.

The insurance company deducted the cost of salvage, which it had insisted upon against the owner's will, from the insured value of the yacht. With the remaining money and the scrap metal value of the wreck the family could scarcely pay for their flights home.

A similar accident occurred to the yacht *Demmy* which ran aground in the winter of 1984 on the Islas Los Roques, 60 miles north of the Venezuelan coast. And she was not insured.

This group of islands extends over an area of roughly 10 by 12 miles and consists of 60 sandy islands, many of them minute, of which only 25 have names. Most of them barely reach 33 ft (10 m) above sea level. Only the main island to the north-west rises to 330 ft (100 m) and it has a lighthouse.

The archipelago is normally only visited by fishermen who work there from temporary quarters. It is also an ideal area for divers and the few anchorages suitable for yachts are idyllic in their remoteness. But, of course, isolated islands are only idyllic when one is visiting them voluntarily and has the means of leaving again. For stranded yachtsmen life on a remote island is somewhat different.

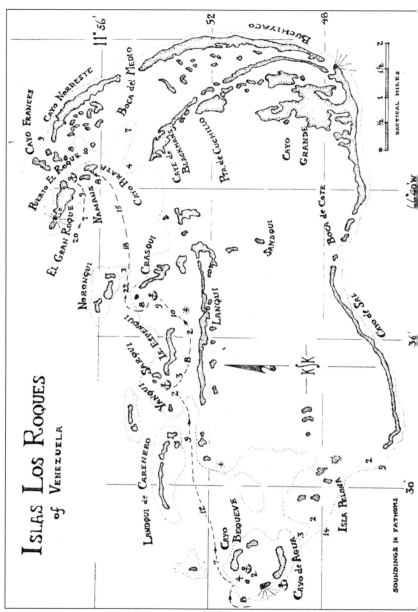

Islas Los Roques off Venezuela. The yacht Demmy ran
ashore near the south-eastern corner of the largely
uninhabited archipelago.

154

*Demmy* is a 44 ft (13.4 m) fibreglass ketch built by her owners, Bernd and Alvart Maierhofer. Her displacement is 12 tons, with a beam of 12 ft 10 in (3.9 m) and a draft of 6 ft 3 in (1.9 m). For the planned circumnavigation she was strongly built, using C-flex, heavy stringers and substantial wooden bulkheads. This sound construction helped to keep the damage to her hull within bounds when she ran aground during the night of 16/17 February 1984, roughly two miles north of the south-east entrance to the archipelago.

*Demmy* was on her way from Isla la Tortuga to the Panama Canal when she struck the reef at 0500 shortly after the watch had changed. The planned course would have taken her clear of the islands, but she was 15 miles off course, mainly due to a strong current. The small fishermen's light that marks one entrance to the lagoon at the south-eastern tip of the islands was not seen due to the prevailing weather.

The heavy surf quickly pushed *Demmy* high on to the reef, assisted by the rising ride. The yacht was pushed over on to her port side where she soon sprang a leak. Was the jagged coral reef going to be *Demmy*'s last resting place? The Maierhofers had invested all they had in the boat which was home for them and their daughters Verena (8) and Yvonne (4).

No matter how bad matters seemed, the Maierhofers did not give up hope. They embarked upon an almost superhuman salvage attempt that took many weeks and had only a very slight chance of success. From the accounts of Alvart and Bernd Maierhofer, of Arthur Schulten of the German yacht *Mermaid* and of Mr and Mrs Pajonk of the Trans Ozean sailing club in Venezuela, I have pieced together the story of the 145 day salvage operation that was assisted by local fishermen and the crews of other yachts.

*1st day after grounding (18 February 1984)* The Maierhofers ferry equipment from the stranded *Demmy* to the nearby island by dinghy. Here they erect a tent in which the family will live in the coming months. After they have taken even the removable ballast to the island the first fishing boats arrive on the scene and offer their assistance. Bernd asks for pulleys, anchors and warps, as well as water and petrol.

*3rd day (20 February)* Using pulleys they manage to pull the bow of the yacht around to face the sea. In the days that follow the two adults try to right the yacht with the help of a car jack and pulleys attached to anchors in order to lie her on her undamaged starboard side.

*8th, 14th and 18th day (25 February, 2 and 6 March)* On all these days *Demmy* falls back on to her port side and has to be righted again.

*22nd day (10 March)* The yacht is now securely upright on her keel and can be carefully leaned over to starboard. The crew begins with the task of slowly pulling her out of the surf, centimetre by centimetre, using pulleys and winches.

*36th day (24 March)* After 150 hours, the required 130 ft (40 m) towards the beach have been covered. Maierhofer now starts to dismantle the interior so that he can repair the 43 sq ft (4 m²) hole on the yacht's port side. Local fishermen sometimes lend a hand and provide the family with food from their catch. Without them Bernd Maierhofer would have despaired long ago. He stays with the boat while his family relax for a few days in Puerto Azul.

*75th day (2 May)* News of the stranding reaches cruising yachts on Martinique. Arthur Schulten's *Mermaid* sets sail for Los Roques to help.

*117th day (13 June)* *Mermaid* arrives in the north of the archipelago and starts to look for *Demmy*.

*121st day (17 June)* *Mermaid* finally reaches *Demmy*. The stranded yacht now lies in 12 in (30 cm) of water about 300 ft (90 m) from the reef, but still 660 ft (200 m) away from deep water. *Mermaid*'s crew find Maierhofer slaving every day under the burning tropical sun as he inches the 12 ton yacht towards deep water. With the aid of a borrowed motor-pump, the coral is cleared from around the keel of the yacht with a crowbar. Then heavy warps tied around the keel are connected via blocks to a set of anchors. The free ends of the warps are led to the yacht's winches. Five hundred turns on the winches move *Demmy* closer to her element by 6 in (15 cm).

But the anchors keep on slipping and only at high tide is it possible to move the yacht at all. Some yards are gained during a period of spring tides but only during the night when there is less swell. The labour of the past months and the constant exposure to water have left their mark on the owner of *Demmy*. He has nasty sores on his legs and without more help, and even more luck, it could take several months for *Demmy* to finally reach deep water again.

*132nd day (28 June)* *Mermaid*'s crew become actively involved in the salvage.

*133rd day (29 June)* *Demmy* is moved 33 ft (10 m) in one night, but next day she is leaking again.

*134th day (30 June)* The hull has to be righted again to repair the leak. The borrowed pump has to be returned the next day.

*135th day (1 July)* The Venezuelan motor yacht *Thalassia* comes to help. The propeller thrust of her dinghy's outboard is used to raise the water level around *Demmy* while the motor yacht, towing with long warps, succeeds in moving her in two stages another 65 ft (20 m), despite neap tides.

*140th day (6 July)* A tug of the Guardia Nacional drags *Demmy* another 330 ft (100 m) over the coral in only 20 in (50 cm) of water. But the price is high; the hull is punctured again in several places and it takes two days of hard work to lean her on to her port side for repairs, using seven anchors.

*143rd day (9 July)* Members of an environmental organization help by widening the channel towards deep water, using their 80 hp outboard. There are now only 33 ft (10 m) left to go.

*144th day (10 July)* The last 33 ft (10 m)! But during the tow, one of *Thalassia*'s two engines is put out of action. Another motor yacht, which happens to be passing, manages the rest. *Demmy* is afloat once more.

*145th day (11 July)* Escorted by *Mermaid* and the French yacht *Zebra*, *Thalassia* tows *Demmy* to Puerto Azul on her remaining engine.

'Now *Demmy* is slipped and the real repairs can start,' Schulten says at the end of his account. 'The Maierhofer family are fit and well, if one disregards the marks left by coral, sun and physical exhaustion. The yacht, on the other hand, is in a sorry state; two severe leaks, one on the port and one on the starboard side, which have been only temporarily patched must now be permanently repaired. The keel is still partly torn open, the interior destroyed. The engine and electrics will have to be completely overhauled after their exposure to salt water. But Alvart and Bernd are full of hope.'

• • • • • • •

## Salvage Shanghai-style

*Raising a sunken yacht from the sea bed tends to be a major operation. Fortunately the cost is usually covered by the insurance policy. In the days when fewer boats had such insurance ingenuity sometimes came to the rescue.*

Towards the end of the 1930s an English yacht was lying in Shanghai, then an extremely busy commercial port. She was moored to a buoy near the bustling harbour. Unfortunately a junk with another in tow hit the yacht and sank her at her moorings.

This caused great embarrassment to the junk owner who was not insured against third party risks. Gesticulating wildly, he conveyed his regret to the owner of the yacht and attempted to convince him that he could raise the yacht himself. Whether he liked the idea or not, the Englishman had to agree in the end as he was unlikely to receive any other compensation. However, he wondered how the other would manage it.

The junk had no gear to lift the wooden yacht. At low water, however, one could stand on her deck with the water up to one's throat. The yacht had both fuel and fresh water tanks which were filled from on deck. At low water the junk owner dived down to the deck, located the filler caps and subsequently unscrewed them. He took both caps into town where he had special replacement caps made with a long, copper tube projecting upwards and a long flexible tube reaching down into the tank. At the next low water he went down to the yacht again, fitted the new caps and was able to pump both tanks dry through the flexible tubes while air was drawn in through the copper tube. In the end the air in both tanks gave enough buoyancy to lift the yacht up to the surface so she could be towed ashore for final repairs.

Nowadays, of course, one would use inflatable buoyancy bags positioned inside or outside the yacht, but if the right equipment is not available creative thinking can often save the situation, as it did in Shanghai.

• • • • • • •

# One-man salvage

*Salvage claims usually arise from the saving of one boat by another, but not always. In this case the salvor, though a yachtsman, was equipped with nothing more than a pair of bathing trunks.*

Seeing an empty yacht, worth nearly £100,000, adrift from her mooring in southern Spain and in imminent danger of going ashore, a yachtsman jumped into the water and swam out to her.

He reached the boat and climbed on board. He tied all her mooring ropes together into one long warp, fastened the end around his chest and swam back to shore. From here he managed to haul the yacht away from the lee shore to a place where he could anchor her safely, keeping the line to the shore as well. He kept an eye on the boat for the next 24 hours.

As he still had not heard from her owner the following day he ordered two heavy cranes to lift the boat out of the water and she was put ashore near the water, professionally laid up on blocks.

The owner only heard about the yacht's unplanned excursion several days later. He then refused to pay salvage to the man who had saved his yacht from probable damage and refused to reimburse him for the cost of the cranes. The case was taken to a court which decided that salvage claims are applicable to yachts and that the salvor does not necessarily have to be at sea to make the claim legitimate. Basically, the court ruled that salvage law applies whenever a vessel is saved by another party. This obviously includes an empty boat in imminent danger of stranding on a rocky shore which is saved by someone swimming out to her.

The man was finally awarded salvage of 10 per cent of the yacht's value, plus the cost of lifting the boat ashore.

# 7
# THE SURVIVORS

---

## Survival stories

*The battle to save a yacht in distress, protracted
as it may be, is sometimes just the prelude to a
much more protracted struggle of the survivors
to save themselves, in a liferaft, on the upturned
hull of their boat, or even alone in the sea. Some
of the longest and most remarkable feats of
survival by yachtsmen are described below.*

Being forced to abandon a yacht at sea is a traumatic experience. Partly it is the fact that the unthinkable has happened
and the boat is gone, for whatever reason. The shock is not
restricted to the period of leaving the yacht and first boarding
the dinghy or liferaft. And it can even prove fatal to someone
who cannot adjust to the new reality. The world in which the
survivors find themselves is exposed to wind, waves and cold
in a way the yacht was not. The physical demands are great
and there is not the chance of even a temporary respite below
decks.

The first essential for survivors is to cope with the sudden
overwhelming sense of isolation and helplessness and to
convert it into a positive attitude towards survival. Imminent
as physical dangers may be, the biggest threat is giving up hope
and giving in to despair.

There are countless examples of humans surviving long periods as castaways, sustained by what nourishment they could get from the sea. What I most admire is their sheer will to survive for hundreds and sometimes thousands of lonely hours. For some the effort must have been almost superhuman as ships had passed by several times before they were finally rescued.

### Three days

The singlehanded sailor Nick Clifton spent three days in 1977 drifting in the Atlantic in a liferaft after his trimaran *Azulao* capsized. He could not stay with the overturned boat but was able to send out a MAYDAY. The liferaft capsized too before he was picked up by a tanker that had been directed to him by the coastguard. The capsized trimaran was eventually washed ashore in England.

### Four days

The solo sailor Jan Gougeon spent four days on his capsized 31 ft (9.45 m) trimaran *Flicka* before a passing ship saw and rescued him. He had been on passage from Bermuda to Newport. His radio beacon failed to transmit a MAYDAY signal.

### Four days

This was also the time that the four survivors of the crew of the catamaran *Jet Services* spent on their boat before they were taken off by helicopter. The large racing catamaran capsized in heavy weather in autumn 1985 while *en route* from the Azores to Brittany, when the leeward hull nosedived below the water. One crew member drowned. The automatic beacon transmitted a distress signal but the rescue craft could not reach the upside-down catamaran through the 40 ft (12 m) waves.

### Seven days

David Hill and Edward Barrett spent seven days on their capsized trimaran 200 miles off the Mexican coast before they were picked up by a passing tanker. They had enough water and food on the boat and were able to use the distress signals from their undamaged emergency pack.

## *Eight days*

Alain Glicksman, his son Denis and three other crew survived eight days in a liferaft, after the 52 ft (16 m) trimaran *RTL Timex* capsized 100 miles north of Bermuda on 10 April 1979 on her way to New York. They spent the first night on their upturned boat, waiting for help that should have been summoned by their radio beacon. But the equipment failed and did not transmit. The next morning they launched the liferaft and tied it to the trimaran but they soon had to cut the painter as staying attached to the yacht was too dangerous. They then drifted for eight days in the raft, sighting five ships who did not see their distress signals. The raft capsized in heavy weather and they had to trim it carefully to keep it upright. The ship that finally picked them up arrived almost too late. Two of them were nearly dead as a result of hypothermia and the other three were at the end of their strength. It was only mutual support that kept them alive, they said later.

## *Eight days*

Three Swiss sailors drifted for eight days in June 1983 in a small liferaft after the trimaran *Manu Kay* capsized in 50 knot winds and high seas a few miles east of Menorca. They had difficulty in freeing the liferaft from underneath the upturned boat in the darkness, and after this effort they got into the raft to rest. The plan was to transfer water, food and other items from the boat to the raft in the morning and remain attached to the boat as long as possible. But in the early hours of the morning the line broke and they drifted helplessly away from the boat without any of the vital equipment.

'We had no water,' one of the crew, André Sörensen, recalls. 'We knew that we needed a certain amount of fluid each day and that we normally digested a certain amount of salt each day in food and drink. So we decided to drink about half a litre of sea water a day.' Drinking sea water is highly controversial in medical circles. The doctor who examined them later found that, 'After eight days of drinking small amounts of sea water they showed no signs of serious dehydration or excessive salt concentration. A few days after their rescue the blood and urine tests were normal.'

The following factors were held to be mainly responsible:

- Calm and disciplined behaviour without excessive movement and thus the minimum loss of water through sweating.

- Draping wet clothes over the skin to lower body temperature and reduce sweating.

- Being in good physical condition to start with. All three were healthy and of average weight with correspondingly high reserves of water in their tissues.

The doctor even assumed that they could have survived for a few days more on salt water, although by then there would have been imminent danger of infection, loss of strength and hallucinations.

But back to the raft. On the morning of the second day they were awoken by a sound that was not the wind and waves. It was a ship. As they opened the canopy and looked outside, their hearts missed a beat; a ship was bearing straight down on them. But instead of running them down, as they had feared, it steamed by only 40 yards away. The small light on top of the raft had gone out three hours after the raft was launched. They had no other means of signalling in the darkness. 'MAYDAY, MAYDAY,' they yelled at the top of their voices but the ship steamed past without noticing them.

Three other ships passed them in the days that followed, none of them seeing the small raft. After the storm passed, the Mediterranean was as calm as a mill pond again but the temperature during the day rose to 104°F (40°C) inside the raft. Small fish lay in the shadow under the raft but the men could not catch them.

They were finally rescued on the evening of the eighth day by a passing yacht.

## Ten days

Four German sailors had to spend ten days in a liferaft after their catamaran *Siddharta* was sunk by a coastal battery on the Spratley Islands in the Chinese Sea. One crew member was killed in the shelling. Another died in the raft. The reason for the attack on the yacht, which occurred on 10 April 1983, is a complete mystery to this day. The yachtsmen were picked up ten days later about 220 miles from the scene of the attack by a Japanese trawler.

### Twelve days

This was the time spent by the Tate family with their children of nine, eleven and twelve years in their liferaft in the Atlantic before they were saved by a Norwegian ship, exhausted but healthy. Their wooden yacht hit an unidentified object while sailing from the Canary Islands to the Caribbean in January 1985. After fighting the rising water level for 12 hours they finally had to abandon the boat 1,000 miles east of Barbados, saving only a limited supply of water and food. Their MAY-DAY calls on VHF and the signals from their EPIRB were evidently not received.

### Twelve days

This was also the time spent by Phillipe Neirynck and Patsy Verwee in an Avon six-man raft after their Atalanta sank in the Bay of Biscay. The Belgian couple had left Falmouth on a favourable forecast on 12 October 1978, bound for Vigo in Spain, but had run into continuously deteriorating weather. After ten days the seas had taken their toll on the wooden hull of the small cruising yacht with its twin ballasted centre-boards. It made water through the centreboard cases faster than could be bailed out. So they eventually had to abandon the boat, and take to the liferaft – two people, a dog, provisions, water and the ship's papers.

'For the next twelve days we were continuously wet,' Neirynck recalls. During the second night in the raft they were extremely frightened too. Breaking seas would flatten the canopy, compressing the rubber tubing under the weight of water. When the water ran off again it would spring back to its original form, only to be compressed again by the next wave.

'We just lay down on the rubber floor and held hands with the dog on our backs. Our nerves were strained and we were afraid of capsizing and losing all our vital equipment. We had fastened ourselves to the raft by our harnesses but we did not know how long it would stand the continuous pounding of the waves. We waited for a freak wave to end it all. In those hours we decided to get married, "until death do us part". But the long dark night passed without accidents and when we awoke next morning the wind and sea had moderated. We were more than glad to be still alive. So we wrote, "Please do not disturb. Just married," in large letters on the raft.'

At least the couple had no problems with water or food. They had taken 9 gallons (40 litres) of water from the boat and drank only a small amount when they really felt thirsty. After twelve days they had only used half their water. Rainwater and dew that was collected from the canopy was stained red (as always on this type of raft) but was still usable as drinking water for the dog.

'Many people asked us later if we would have killed the dog as a last resort to survive,' Neirynck recalls, 'but we never even considered it. We thought it natural that he should have the same chance of survival as ourselves, with no extra privileges but no fewer rights.'

As Verwee opened the canopy one morning on a calm sea they saw a huge tanker some way off. They fired their last distress rocket and signalled SOS on their torch but after five minutes the batteries were exhausted. The big ship did not signal back but nor did it move away. Long moments of uncertainty followed, but after one-and-a-half hours the ship was still there about one mile off, waiting for the raft to drift down to it.

At 0930 Neirynck and Verwee, together with their dog Yeti, are all safe aboard the Liberian tanker with its French crew. 'They had seen our rocket,' Neirynck explains, 'but it took them several hours to manoeuvre the giant ship close to us. They reckon that they were about seven miles away when they saw the rocket. But it was only due to our signals with the torch that they were actually able to locate us. The radar only picked up the raft after they had come within a mile of us.'

### Eighteen days

This was how long Wolfgang Kraker von Schwarzenfeld fought for his life after his trimaran capsized on an Atlantic crossing roughly 1,200 miles east of New York on 22 July

1957. The young German, who in 1955 had been one of the first to cross the Atlantic in a catamaran, was finally rescued by a cargo ship 1,400 miles east of New York.

He described the time spent on his upturned boat, like no other shipwrecked sailor before or after him, talking about the thirst, the hunger, the cold, being constantly soaked, about the bitter disappointment of being between two ships that passed each other on either side of him, wishing each other a good trip on the Morse lamp over his head, about the fruitless attempts to catch fish and the battles with sharks, the pains in his joints, the suppurating sores and the many hours of hallucinations.

On 8 August he was more dead than alive. He lay in the miniature inflatable dinghy which was tied between the main hull and outrigger and had made his peace with himself and the world. The sea was flat calm but he had decided not to try and catch fish any more nor scoop up sea water with his hand to drink. His breathing was deep and relaxed. He closed his eyes and drifted off to sleep. But then his eyelids quivered, he opened his eyes ... and saw a ship.

'Don't get excited,' he told himself, for he feared that this one would steam past without noticing him like all the others before. The disappointment would kill him instantly.

But his instinct for survival won once more. He climbed on to the hull of the capsized boat, untied the yellow rubber dinghy and lifted it up as far as his diminished strength would allow. The ship stopped. The crew took him on board. 'Never will I forget how wretched I . . . ,' he whispers before he faints. Fortunately for him he can't hear the men joking, 'Shall we throw him back in straight away? He won't make it, anyway.' But he did make it and he was put ashore a week later in Monrovia.

### Twenty-six days
In February 1979 Elmo Wortmann and his daughters Cindy (16), Jena (12) and his son Randy (15) survived for 26 days on a frozen rock off Alaska after their cruiser *Homer* had stranded on the southern tip of the island, known as Long Island. They had set sail from Canada the day before on a short coastal cruise, but had to fight for their lives for 26 days

on a lonely rock, on the border between land and sea, with only a leaking dinghy, a box of matches and a wet sail. For three weeks they lived off algae and mussels before they built a raft and began to make their way northwards to the next inhabited island. They arrived with severe frostbite and only just won their race against death.

## Twenty-eight days

In the summer of 1976 the skipper of the American ketch *Spirit* survived for 28 days on a liferaft after the 42 ft (12.8 m) yacht had hit a floating object, probably a half-submerged container, roughly 500 miles off the coast of California, sinking immediately. The crew of five didn't have time to activate the emergency transmitter but they did have two liferafts. Two of the crew got into one raft and were picked up by a ship 21 days later. The skipper, Bruce Collins, got into the other raft with the remaining two crew but both of them died within two days. One was buried at sea. The other body was still in the raft when Collins was found in a search that had been triggered by the rescue of the other two. Collins had spent most of his time asleep and said, 'Luckily there was a lot of rain so I could catch a bit of water now and again.'

## Thirty-seven days

Lyn and Dougal Robertson, together with their children Douglas (18), twins Neil and Sandy (12) and friend Robin Williams (22), had to survive 37 days after their yacht *Lucette* was sunk by killer whales on 15 June 1972 in the Pacific near the Galapagos Islands.

For the first 19 days of their ordeal they had a liferaft and a small open dinghy at their disposal so that they could at least lie down and sleep in turns. But the rubber raft gradually disintegrated and could not be kept afloat even with the greatest determination. Finally all six persons had to transfer to the tiny 9 ft 4 in (2.85 m) dinghy which then only had a freeboard of 6 in (15 cm).

For the following 18 days they had to survive by constantly trimming the boat to avoid being swamped by a wave and sunk, catching rainwater and fish and doing everything else while cramped into this minute space. And all the time they headed for the coast hundreds of miles away. When they were finally picked up by a Japanese fishing boat they had covered 750 miles from where the yacht was sunk.

## Forty-two days

William Hoadley (36) and Debbie Blocker (20), who was pregnant, left Guanaja, Honduras, in a seaworthy 49 ft (15 m) motor yacht on 27 May 1973, bound for the United States. For the first two days the trip was uneventful. But then the fuel pipes clogged up. But after Hoadley had cleaned and replaced them the engines would not start as the batteries were too low.

The yacht was about 80 miles south of Cuba. With bed clothes, boathooks, oars and blankets they made a jury-rig but even this could not prevent the ensuing 42 day drift. The Gulf Stream took the yacht through the Yucatan Channel into the Gulf of Mexico. 'Then we drifted from the Cuban coast toward the Mississippi delta,' Hoadley recalls. 'The current from the mighty river then took hold of us and pushed us back to the Yucatan peninsula where we were again picked up by the Gulf Stream that pushed us back north.' Despite her jury-rig, *Tahoma* was a helpless object at the mercy of the elements and currents. Their distress signals were not seen by passing ships until they were finally picked up by a tug 60 miles southeast of the mouth of the Mississippi. During their involuntary 1,500-mile voyage they survived on rainwater and fish, as the provisions on board lasted only for the first couple of days.

## Forty-six days

This was how long the American John Liebespeck (44), his son Martin (19) and Christian Guilmoto (28) were adrift in their leaking, crippled 30 ft (9 m) yacht *Little Arch* in the Pacific in January 1980 before they were rescued by a passing ship. They had embarked upon a voyage from Hawaii to the Marshall Islands which normally would have taken them about 18 days.

The first gale they encountered smashed the rudder; the second one only a few days later started a leak; and the third broke the mast, swept the dinghy off the deck and made the leak worse. When the provisions were used up the three survived on a dolphin and several sharks which they caught, and rain water. They needed all the strength they could muster to keep pumping out the leaking yacht. Compared to other crews that have had to survive in liferafts, their situation may have been a little easier, but they proved in an impressive way how you can survive on a crippled yacht, following the important maxim of not leaving the boat before she leaves you.

### Fifty-five days (voluntary)

George Siegler and Charles Gore spent 55 days in 1974 in a 16 ft (4.8 m) inflatable dinghy as an experiment in surviving several weeks at sea and to demonstrate that inflatables are a useful alternative to liferafts, having the advantage of being steerable. They also wanted to test a new diet, specially developed for survivors, in a realistic environment.

On 4 July they left the Golden Gate Bridge bound for Hawaii in their inflatable *Courageous* that had only a pair of oars for propulsion. Their food consisted mainly of 3.3 lbs (1.5 kg) of specially made sugar cane tablets which were purported to deliver maximum energy and could be taken without water. They also had a desalinator that could produce about one pint (0.6 litre) of fresh water daily which would be combined with a third of a pint (0.2 litre) of sea water for their daily ration of liquids. The salt water, which would provide them with necessary minerals, was drunk first, the bitter taste of the salt then being washed away with the fresh water. The only problem associated with this diet was slight indigestion.

Their survival pack had an overall weight of only 18 lbs (8 kg). An important part of it was vitamin tablets, while the rest consisted of a first aid kit, a waterproof torch, flares, compass, knife, hooks and line and a sheet for collecting rain water.

The dinghy capsized 120 miles off the American coast in 35 knots of wind and the men had serious difficulty in righting it again. The food in their survival pack lasted them for 40 days. After that, the two voluntary castaways began to obtain food from the sea – two birds and five fish to begin with. For navigation they used only a wristwatch with a timer that enabled them to determine the length of the day from sunrise to sunset.

With this figure and a graph they were able to establish their latitude to within 30 miles. By dividing the same figure by two and then adding a correction factor for the time of sunrise they were further able to pinpoint their longitude to within five miles. For emergency navigation this striking system is surely accurate enough.

The two men reached their destination, Hawaii, in 55 days. They both had lost weight – Charles Gore from 168 lbs (76 kg) to 126 lbs (57 kg), George Siegler from 183 lbs (83 kg) to 128 lbs (58 kg). Apart from that, they were weak but healthy. The most important result of their voyage was that they had shown that a rectangular raft could be made to drift or sail on a specified course towards the nearest land, using paddles, oars, sails or whatever. This of course is not the case with the current round liferafts. In a round raft the Baileys had to drift passively for 117 days. In contrast, Dougal Robertson and his family were able to make progress towards the American coast in their heavily overladen dinghy. In a proper ship's longboat, an open boat 23 ft (7 m) long with 18 people on board, Captain Bligh managed to sail 3,500 miles across the Pacific to safety after the mutiny on the *Bounty*.

## *Sixty-five days (voluntary)*

The French doctor Alain Bombard spent 65 days as a voluntary castaway in 1952 in his inflatable dinghy *l'Hérétique*, crossing the Atlantic from the Canary Islands to Barbados. He wanted to prove his theories on survival at sea in practice and demonstrate that a human being does not have to starve or die of thirst at sea.

Bombard managed to catch rainwater and fish with very little equipment, obtaining his daily requirement of vitamins from plankton, and healing skin sores by sheer will-power. A small, much-repaired sail carried him along. The many physical and mental crises that arose on the voyage tested him beyond the limit of what had seemed to be humanly possible.

At the time Bombard's was an unparalleled feat of survival which nevertheless came in for some criticism. Today key elements of Bombard's survival tactics are included in the survival training given to professional seamen. His ideas have also proved vital for shipwrecked yachtsmen such as Alain Glicksman and Steven Callahan.

### Seventy-three days

Bob Tinienko (35) survived for 73 days in a trimaran that capsized on 10 July 1972 about 200 miles out into the Pacific from San Francisco. All electrical equipment was destroyed in the capsize so he could not transmit a distress call. The main water tank and the watermaker were rendered useless. After 26 days his pregnant wife Linda died. After 73 days Tinienko and his friend Jim Fisher were rescued but Fisher died shortly afterwards in hospital.

### Seventy-five days

This is the time that the Swiss singlehanded sailor Eric Steiner survived on his ketch *Le Perfier* in 1976 after the boat had capsized on a trip from the Marquesas Islands to Sydney, losing both masts and sustaining severe damage to the engine. Luckily he had taken on board water and provisions for 50 days which he eked out for the 75 days of his ordeal.

### Seventy-six days

The American singlehanded sailor Steve Callahan had to survive 76 days in a tiny liferaft in 1982. He was bound for the Caribbean from Hierro in the Canary Islands in his 21 ft (6.5 m) cruising yacht *Napoleon Solo* when, seven days out, the boat suddenly started to make water and sank quickly. He only had time to inflate the liferaft and jump into it with an emergency grab bag, a knife and a few tools. In the darkness he seized anything floating from the sinking boat – a cabbage, a mug, the danbuoy. He cut off a piece of the mainsail to wrap around himself to withstand the cold as he was wearing nothing but a T-shirt and his wrist-watch. As *Napoleon Solo* was still afloat, though half-submerged, he retrieved a sodden sleeping bag and a pillow. He planned to return to the boat after daybreak to salvage some water canisters and more food, stowed in watertight plastic containers. He also had hopes of perhaps finding the leak and mending it, but during the night the line to the boat broke and Callahan drifted away in the raft.

Mentally he took stock of his situation: 'Water: about a gallon, maybe two if I can get some fresh fish. Solid food: about three pounds. The raft: in good shape. Distance to the nearest shipping lanes: 450 miles. Conclusion: without additional food or water I shall be very lucky to reach the shipping lanes.'

A castaway can normally survive for about ten days without water – without food, about 30 days. Although Callahan was in an area devoid of shipping, he hoped to be in the shipping lanes in less than 40 days. The EPIRB was transmitting continuously, but as he celebrated his thirtieth birthday with two ounces (50 g) of peanuts and half a pint (0.4 l) of water, it had transmitted for 36 hours without apparent result and had exhausted its battery.

Callahan was lucky to have had three devices for making drinking water. These used solar energy to produce up to a pint of drinking water a day from seawater. But only one of them worked, the other two proving to be useless. One pint of water is not much in hot weather and he started to think about catching rainwater. 'The main problem is that the canopy of the raft is painted orange and all the water flowing off it is made undrinkable by the paint. But I used the defective water filters with a bit of sailcloth to catch rainwater.'

Callahan spent most of his time in the sleeping bag. After 40 days he reached the shipping lanes, but, he says, 'I drifted right across the shipping lanes without being noticed. I saw several ships (two of them passed as little as a mile away) but they did not notice me. My distress flares were obviously useless, maybe because they were fired by day. On the other hand I could see no one on the decks of either ship.'

His most important piece of survival equipment had by now become the harpoon which he grabbed by chance when leaving the boat. He managed to harpoon a dorado fish from among the shoal that usually accompanied him, so he was able to eat up to four pounds (2 kg) of raw fish a day. This may not be everyone's favourite dish but the inner organs of a dorado contain many essential vitamins. The eyes and minute cavities in the spine contain fluid, while the liver and the roe actually do not taste that bad.

173

*American singlehanded yachtsman Steve Callahan who*
*survived for 76 days on a liferaft after his boat* Napoleon
Solo *sank west of the Canary Islands.*

On the forty-third day the harpoon broke. A fish took the
spear into the depths of the ocean. Moreover, it also ripped the
bottom of the raft. The rubber tube now lost air continuously.
Callahan worked for a whole week, trying to repair the raft,
but the patch he put over the leak always came off again. Then
he had the idea of sewing it as well. It took him several days of
painstaking labour but in the end the raft was airtight again.
He regards this as a turning point in his ordeal. 'I was near to
death, very desperate, but I came through it.'

After ten weeks the castaway had stopped counting the
days. He lived from one day to the next. But even in these deso-
late times he still noted the course of his drift and tried to keep
some sort of dead reckoning of his position. He judged his
course from the direction of sunrise and sunset, estimated the
speed of his drift in relation to passing clumps of seaweed, and
calculated latitude with a 'sextant' made from three pencils
lashed together. He knew the ocean currents from the chart,
and got new hope as he noticed the water's change of colour
and the different species of fish now escorting him. He was
over the continental shelf.

174

One night he woke up and saw lights, perhaps even the flashing of a lighthouse. With daybreak the 'hallucination' became wonderful reality. Callahan could see an island with buildings, and soon he heard an outboard motor coming close. A flock of birds had gathered over his raft and some fishermen were hoping to find a large school of fish where they eventually found the raft. They took Callahan back to the island, Marie Galante in the French Antilles.

The 76 day drift 'probably set the record for the slowest-ever Atlantic crossing' as Callahan puts it. Above all, he says, 'I have been very lucky to survive, by having been in good physical shape and the raft holding together for so long. I thank Nature for the variety of food to be got from the ocean and to have been given a new life. Perhaps other sailors will be inspired by my experience to see life at sea with different eyes.'

*Steve Callahan photographed with fishermen who rescued him close to the island of Marie Galante in the French Antilles.*

He adds, 'I am convinced that I would not have survived with just the standard equipment on the liferaft. My survival was 80 per cent attributable to the contents of my personal grab bag and 20 per cent to the raft's equipment. The standard fishing equipment included with the raft, for instance, is not enough to survive with. Only because I am a keen sports fisherman did I carry a harpoon on the boat. And it was only because the boat was so small and I did not know where to stow this bulky piece of equipment that I packed it in my grab bag. Ultimately it saved my life!'

## One hundred and eighteen days

The time that Maralyn and Maurice Bailey spent on a liferaft and an inflatable dinghy after their yacht *Auralyn* had been sunk by a whale 300 miles north-east of the Galapagos islands in March 1973 is the longest that yachtsmen have ever survived at sea. With a raft and a dinghy the couple had the same amount of space available as the six-person Robertson family in the same area, but they had to survive for three times as long.

Physically, they managed to survive by perfecting their technique for catching rainwater and, with sharpened senses, by catching fish and turtles with the most primitive gear imaginable. Some of the turtles were tied to the outside of the raft or dinghy as a living food larder. But it is still astonishing that they were able to cope with skin ailments, weight loss and problems connected with their unbalanced diet for such a long time.

The anguish when, one after another, eight ships passed them without noticing their distress signals is even harder to imagine. How much they had made a world for themselves of the sea, the fish, the birds and the turtles was described by Maurice Bailey after they were finally picked up, after nearly four months, by a Korean fishing boat. 'Maralyn is still waving her lifejacket at the ship that is already showing us her stern. It is the first ship that we have seen in 43 days. "Come back," Maralyn cries. "Please!" Kneeling in the dinghy at the time I have already lost interest in the ship that Maralyn is still imploring to come back. "Stay away," I think. "This is our world now – the sea, the fish, the birds and the turtles." Maralyn has suddenly stopped crying and begging. But she is still waving at the ship. I look up at the ship for a moment. Is it coming towards us or are my eyes deceiving me? Maralyn looks at me with moist eyes. "It is coming back," she says. And it was coming back!'

## Towed for four hours

Yachtsman Leonard Delmas was towed behind his 34 ft (10.35 m) yacht *Another Girl* for four hours on 20 September 1971. He had left the St Francis Yacht Club on San Francisco Bay at 1930 to return by boat to his home in Marin County, about a mile and a half east of the Golden Gate Bridge. He was in a bit of a hurry so he set the sails while motoring at full speed. He was 41 years old, physically fit and an experienced sailor, but completely unprepared for what was to follow.

He was in the middle of the bay, still motorsailing, relaxed and leaning back against the guard rails, steering with the tiller extension, when the lifeline broke and he fell backwards into the sea. Luckily the mainsheet was caught around his foot, attaching him to the boat which now tacked but still motored on at full throttle. He was now being towed behind the yacht at 5 knots. The water was fairly cold and there was no other vessel in sight in the darkness. He had two options. He could let go and try to swim ashore. Or he could hang on to the boat. He decided to stay with the boat and try to get back on board.

But his attempts to climb on board ended in failure. All he could do was pull himself up the stern of the boat so he could just reach the toe rail with his outstretched hand. Once he managed to pull himself up on the mounting bracket of the lifebuoy, but when he got to deck level the fitting broke and he fell back into the water. Now he was suspended under the exhaust outlet but he managed to pull out more sheet so he was clear of the fumes.

After an hour of desperately clinging to the thin line that cut into his hands, he tied it around his arm and chest, only to be pulled under water. So he had to resume his grip on the line again. By now the yacht was motoring in circles around the bay but unfortunately not attracting any attention. Soon two hours had passed and he felt his strength diminishing. His unbelievable predicament was driving him crazy, but he did not want to die so there was nothing for it but to hang on to the line and hope for the best. After another hour he noticed that the boat was now heading for the passenger boat harbour where the large passenger launches are moored at a safe distance from the shore. He now expected the yacht to collide with one of the launches and had just made up his mind to let go and swim to one of the other boats, when the yacht stopped miraculously without the crash of a collision. She had run into one of the mooring lines and her engine kept her in position as if she was moored there.

It took Delmas another 30 minutes to climb via the mooring line on to a passenger launch. After nearly four hours in the water he at last had a solid deck beneath his feet, but his problems were not entirely over, seriously cold now on the deck of the launch and still far from the shore. He had no choice but to pull his yacht gingerly towards him, climb back on board and return to where he had set off from, the St Francis Yacht Club.

Delmas has drawn the same conclusions from this near-fatal accident as other yachtsmen, particularly singlehanded ones, have drawn before him – always wear a harness when sailing alone, tow a line astern and, most important, never use the guard rail as a backrest. His account ends: 'Every yachtsman should be prepared for the unexpected at all times. He should never lose his nerve, not even in a seemingly hopeless situation. Above all, don't panic!'

## Swimming for seven hours

On his way from Tahiti to Hawaii the singlehanded sailor Fred Wood was swept off the deck of his boat *Windsong* by the boom when she gybed accidentally and found himself in the water roughly five miles from Christmas Island. Luckily Wood was a good swimmer and reached the island by swimming for seven hours, miraculously passing unscathed through the sharp coral reefs surrounding it. On the outer beach of the atoll he survived for 15 days during which time he built a raft to cross the lagoon. He lived on coconuts and small crabs. He never saw his boat again.

## Swimming for eight hours

Colin Haskin (34) was in the water for eight hours after his boat had collided with an anchored ship on the American Pacific coast in a force 9 in the spring of 1982. The yacht sank quickly and two other crew members drowned. Haskin swam for the shore three miles away in 20 ft (6 m) waves. In reply to the question of where he found the strength for this incredible feat he said, 'I thought of all those things that I still wanted to do in my life.'

## Swimming for twenty-four hours

In the summer of 1985 singlehanded yachtsman Egon Purkl (36) survived in the Mediterranean for no less than 24 hours after he had fallen off his 20 ft (6 m) cruiser *Skarabäus* about 30 miles north-west of the island of Stromboli.

The sea was calm as he went forward to clear the furling line of the genoa. He was wearing light summer clothes with neither a harness nor a lifejacket. As he was alone the tiller was lashed and the yacht was steering herself. He was not trailing a lifeline which would at least have given him a theoretical chance of getting back on board. When he fell in the sea he found that he could not swim as fast as the boat, even in light airs. So his situation seemed hopeless as the boat sailed away, alone in an empty sea without a lifejacket.

He was lucky that the sea was warm with a temperature of 79°F (26°C). He had, theoretically, about 20 hours before he died of hypothermia. Moreover, it is easier to stay afloat in the Mediterranean with its high salinity of 3.5 per cent than in the ocean. But Purkl knew that the coast of Stromboli was 30 miles away, too far to reach by swimming.

Then he had a stroke of luck; close by he saw the floating remains of a fishing net, including two small plastic buoys. He was able to tie them to his arms or legs in the ensuing hours to avoid cramp and rest a little.

The first ship passed a couple of hours later, about two miles away and of course unable to see him. Then dolphins arrived but did not stay with him long. He swam through the night suffering badly from the cold and conserving energy as much as possible. The next day another school of dolphins arrived and he saw another ship on the horizon. He had already nearly given up hope when he noticed that the ship had altered course towards him. A boat was lowered and he was rescued.

His rescue was made possible by the dolphins. The watch-keeper on the ship had been looking at them through binoculars when he suddenly saw Purkl's head bobbing in the water.

After first aid on the ship and a few days in hospital Purkl embarked on the search for his boat which had been salvaged by an Italian yachtsman.

• • • • • • •

# Liferafts: a fatal weakness

*Numerous cases have been recorded of liferaft painters breaking before they were meant to, with varying results. Sometimes it even proved to be beneficial. But there seems little doubt that the consequences could as easily be fatal.*

The makers of Beaufort liferafts describe how an American yachtsman had to abandon his sinking boat. After he had recovered from the first shock of the collision and surprise that the container on deck, on which he had sometimes sat during past weeks, had actually transformed itself into a liferaft, he decided that he would take as many items with him in the raft as possible.

So he went into the cabin and took the most important items, among them water cans, food, bottles of fruit juice. These were followed by duvets, pillows and clothes, all of which he threw into the cockpit. When he realized that he still had more time left he started to dismantle the radio and sat-nav, and put the searchlight out in the cockpit and a pair of batteries to power it.

He thought of his two new sails which he would not want to lose, and the sextant. Then he remembered another vital item – the first aid kit. But he got another shock as he went back into the cockpit; the liferaft had floated away.

This slightly tongue-in-cheek account does not tell us how the man was eventually saved. Perhaps the damaged part of the hull came out of the water due to transferring so much weight into the cockpit.

British yachtsmen Steve Dalton and John Webb were forced to stay on board their yacht *Lennoxen* after running into a severe autumnal gale in the Bay of Biscay, roughly 250 miles south-west of Brest, in October 1984 and being dismasted in 50 knots of wind. Unnerved by the wind and sea they launched their liferaft which inflated instantly. But the painter broke before they could board the raft. In the end this proved a stroke of luck as they eventually got back to Brest a few days later under engine.

The German sailor Wolfgang Quix ran aground on the North Sea coast between the rivers Jade and Weser in September 1985. With him were his wife and young son. They were going to be winched off the liferaft by a helicopter. The raft was to be still attached to the stranded yacht by its painter, but it broke and the raft drifted away.

In 1983 three Swiss sailors were involuntarily separated from their boat after their trimaran *Manu Kay* capsized west of Menorca. They had tied the raft by means of a 13 ft (4 m) long painter to the mast of the upturned multihull while they were resting inside the raft, planning to salvage some vital gear from the boat in the morning. But the painter broke during the night and they drifted away from the boat.

The painter of another liferaft broke after the capsize of the catamaran *Apache Sundancer* on the last leg of the Round Britain Race in 1970. This multihull also stayed afloat, proving a much easier target for searching ships and aircraft, as well as a store of vital equipment, food and water.

The same thing happened to Bill Quenlan and his nephew David Lucas in 1978 when their 40 ft (12 m) trimaran overturned in the Pacific 500 miles off the Mexican coast. Again the painter attaching the liferaft to the upturned boat broke. After drifting away from the boat, the raft capsized several times in the rough seas before the weather settled again. After five days the food and drink in the raft had been nearly used up. It was then that Bill Quenlan jumped overboard, sacrificing his life to save that of his nephew who was able to survive on the remaining provisions until he was picked up by a fishing boat some days later.

Similarly, the two crew of the Hartley trimaran that capsized in June 1972 off New Zealand were separated from the boat when the painter of the liferaft parted. Luckily the raft was sighted a few days later by a fishing boat which picked up the two sailors.

The American singlehanded sailor Steve Callahan, who survived an incredible 76 days in his raft, was also parted from his boat by a broken painter, before he could salvage important survival equipment from her.

There are other examples of liferafts that have broken free prematurely. All liferaft manufacturers design the painter to break under a certain load. The idea, of course, is that the raft should not be pulled down by the boat as she sinks. But, as the above examples show, the weak link can be a danger in itself if it is *too* weak and this was the case with some yacht liferafts.

# INDEX